TOUCHED WITH FIRE

LONDON : GEOFFREY CUMBERLEGE
OXFORD UNIVERSITY PRESS

OLIVER WENDELL HOLMES, JR.

Touched With Fire

CIVIL WAR LETTERS AND DIARY

OF

OLIVER WENDELL HOLMES, JR.

1861–1864

EDITED BY

MARK DE WOLFE HOWE

HARVARD UNIVERSITY PRESS
CAMBRIDGE, MASSACHUSETTS
1947

THROUGH OUR GREAT GOOD FORTUNE, IN
OUR YOUTH OUR HEARTS WERE TOUCHED
WITH FIRE.

Mr. Justice Holmes,
Memorial Day Address, 1884.

THIS PREFACE would not be an appropriate place for an examination of the influence which the Civil War had upon the thought and attitude of Mr. Justice Holmes. Much, if not all, of the contemporaneous meaning which the War had for him is indicated in the letters to his parents and in the diary of his last two months of military service. The contemporaneous meaning, however, is not the only significant meaning and it may well be that of the two wars, the war in fact and the war in retrospect, it was the latter which was dominantly formative of his philosophy. That question, however, could not profitably be discussed on the basis of the materials in this volume alone. The letters and diary constitute the record of three vivid years of experience and speak for themselves. Perhaps if they were being published at a different time in our history their editor would feel obliged to remind the reader of the doubts and enthusiasms which accompany all young men at war. Today, however, that reminder would be superfluous. The language and technique of war have changed since 1861, but the influence of wars both total and less than total upon the minds of those who fight them has not been appreciably different. This record, if it has no other significance, has that, and one suspects that Holmes would not be sorry that his earliest and simplest expression of feeling and belief will serve to bring that truth home.

.

In February, 1942, the late John Gorham Palfrey, literary executor of the estate of Mr. Justice Holmes, requested me to undertake the preparation of the official biography of the Justice. The work was to be official only in the sense that I was to be given access to all of the Justice's personal papers. At the time when this arrangement was made Mr. Palfrey turned over to me a substantial number of Holmes's letters, on the understanding that the question of their eventual utilization would be determined later. It was contemplated that certain groups of the letters might most appropriately be published separately and that others might be absorbed in the biography. The years of war interrupted progress on the papers, and it was not until the winter of 1945-1946, after Mr. Palfrey's death, that a systematic examination of the bulk of the papers became possible.

Various indications had led to the belief that none of Justice Holmes's Civil War letters to his parents had been preserved. Mr. Palfrey and I had, therefore, assumed that there would be great difficulties in the preparation of an authentic account of his Civil War experience. It was, accordingly, a considerable surprise when the letters and diary herein reproduced were discovered at the bottom of one of the boxes in which the Justice's papers had been kept. It was evident that both

Holmes and his mother had gone over the letters carefully some time after the Civil War, for the envelopes of the majority contain notations in Mrs. Holmes's handwriting describing the contents of the letters, and a large number of the envelopes also carry similar notes in the Justice's hand. The large gaps in the correspondence, and one or two annotations by the Justice, make it reasonably clear that he destroyed an appreciable number of his letters to his family. So far as I know, none of the Civil War letters of Dr. and Mrs. Holmes, or of their children, to Holmes have been preserved.

On the inside cover of the diary there is the heading "Vol. II." This, together with references in the letters to an earlier diary, makes it clear that Holmes in his first period of service with the 20th Regiment, from the summer of 1861 to the winter of 1863-1864, had kept a brief record of day to day events. That earlier diary has not, however, been found among his papers and the belief seems justified that, with the exception of a few pages, it was destroyed by him. Those few pages describing his wounding at Ball's Bluff were loosely inserted in the front of Volume II and are reproduced herein.

If this interpretation of the Justice's disposition of his Civil War letters and diaries is warranted, it may properly be said that he was himself the editor of this volume. He at least made the initial determination of which letters and records were worthy of preservation and himself eliminated those which he did not care to have other eyes see. This, of course, has reduced my problem to a minimum and has made my responsibility more clerical than editorial. In my annotations I have attempted merely to make the running account in letters and diary comprehensible to a generation unfamiliar with details concerning the events and persons described. Though it would have been easy to put the documents in dress uniform and add spit and polish to the battle dress in which the originals were clothed, I have made no alterations or omissions in the text; the informalities of punctuation and abbreviation are preserved. To have altered form in such matters would, I believe, have appreciably affected substance.

Military historians of the Civil War will, I very much fear, find deficiencies, if not inaccuracies, in the annotations. I hope, however, that my initial ignorance has been an advantage to the general reader, for it has led me to seek for those supplementary facts which seemed essential for understanding. If experts want more, their proficiency will, I feel sure, give them better guidance than I could have offered.

My warmest thanks are owing to Miss Anne Warren whose painstaking assistance in the accurate preparation of the manuscript greatly simplified my task.

MARK DE WOLFE HOWE

Cambridge, Massachusetts
18 September, 1946

Contents

LETTERS, MAY 1—OCTOBER 23, 1861   1

DIARY, BALL'S BLUFF   21

LETTERS, MARCH 1862—DECEMBER 1862   35

LETTERS, MARCH 1863—APRIL 1864   83

DIARY AND LETTERS, MAY 3—JULY 1864   99

Illustrations

OLIVER WENDELL HOLMES, JR.   *Frontispiece*

*From an undated photograph reproduced by courtesy of the
Massachusetts Commandery of the Loyal Legion.*

STAFF OFFICERS, 20TH REGIMENT MASSACHUSETTS
VOLUNTEERS   12

*From a photograph taken in the summer of 1861, reproduced
by courtesy of the Massachusetts Commandery of the Loyal
Legion. The officers, from left to right, are: Major Paul J.
Revere, Adjutant Charles L. Peirson, Surgeon Henry Bryant,
Colonel William R. Lee, Lieutenant Colonel Francis W. Pal-
frey, First Lieutenant Charles W. Folsom, Assistant Surgeon
Nathan Hayward.*

OLIVER WENDELL HOLMES, JR.   80

*From an undated photograph found among his personal papers.
The absence of insignia of rank suggests that it was taken in
the spring of 1861 when Holmes was training as a Private in
the Fourth Battalion.*

SIXTH CORPS HEADQUARTERS AT COLD HARBOR,
JUNE 1, 1864   136

*The following identification of officers is based upon Thomas
W. Hyde, Following the Greek Cross, or Memories of the
Sixth Army Corps (Boston, 1894), p. 210. Back row: Captain
Whittlesey, Captain Haydn, Captain Holmes (with black felt
hat), Major Whittier, Colonel Tompkins (with beard), Colonel
Franklin, Major Tompkins, Captain Russell. Front row: Dr.
Bland, Colonel Hyde, Captain McClellan, Dr. Holman, General
Wright, Major Farrar, Captain Halsted (with sword), Colonel
Kent, Colonel Manning.*

LETTERS, MAY 1—OCTOBER 23, 1861

My Dear Mother

I have just time to write you a word that I'm in bully condition and have got to enjoying the life much —I've a slight cold in the head but not annoying. I've had my hair cut by a combination of G. Perry[2] and Niles[3] in regular Jail-bird stile.[4]

[1] In April Holmes had withdrawn from the Senior class at Harvard College and had enlisted as a Private in the New England Guards, a Boston unit of the Massachusetts Volunteer Militia, commonly designated as the Fourth Battalion. On April 25, 1861, following a vote of the Battalion to undertake guard duty without pay at Fort Independence in Boston Harbor, the Battalion went through a course of basic training under the command of Captain T. G. Stevenson. Stevenson, when Brigadier General commanding the 1st Division of the Ninth Corps, was killed at Spottsylvania. All records of the New England Guards since 1845 were destroyed in the Boston fire of 1872. It is accordingly difficult to ascertain details concerning the organization. See James B. Gardner, "The New England Guards," *Bostonian Society Publications,* IV (1907), 9.

[2] Perhaps George B. Perry, later First Lieutenant, 20th Regiment Massachusetts Volunteers.

[3] Not identified.

[4] It has been reported that Dr. Holmes visited Fort Independence at the time of this or a similar incident. See Alfred S. Roe, *The Twenty-Fourth Regiment Massachusetts Volunteers, 1861-1866* (Worcester, Mass., 1907), p. 11.

Send me of the fat of the land. Several *lbs*. of butter would be a good thing—also fresh meat, olives &c. as per previous advices—I want a *carpet bag* with *hdkfs*, towels, and plenty of space in it—Send the big one—quickly.

O W H

[September 8, 1861]
Camp Kalorama[1]

Dear Mother

Here we are, safe and well—We got a late dinner the day after starting at New York (Read an account of it in papers before we had sat down) I dined with some of the fellows at Delmonico's (not in the barracks—) Breakfast next morn at Phil^a Took till night to get to Baltimore & arrived in the morning (yesterday) at Washington.

The passage you see was very long and there was very little sleep or food—Rather enjoyed it for all though—Last night got to camp—much work to find things & of course a waggon wheel had smashed my trunk I have

---

[1] On July 10, 1861, following his graduation from Harvard College, Holmes was commissioned First Lieutenant in Company A of the 20th Regiment Massachusetts Volunteers, one of the "three-year" regiments. The Regiment was in training at Camp Massasoit, Readville, Mass., during the summer of 1861, was mustered into the Federal service on August 8, and left Readville for Washington on September 4. It arrived in Washington on the morning of September 7 and marched to Camp Kalorama, at Georgetown Heights, where it encamped on the evening of the same day.

bent it back so that it is serviceable however though its beauty is fled forever—My Brandy flask was pulverized. After much anxiety however most things have been found & hereafter each C° has a waggon and there will be more order—Hereafter too I think we shall have enough to eat & have seen the worst in way of hardships unless on special occasions. There is expectation of a fight very soon but we I do not believe run any chance of service except perhaps as reserve.

The carpet bag was an invaluable dodge.

The man has just called for letters so that you may hear something. I'll seal this up & write again in more leisure

Yours with millions of love for Father & A. & N.[2]

My Darling

O. W. Holmes, Jr.

Send my poem[3] after Wright[4] & Pomeroy[5] to C. Walton,[6] care M. L. Hallowell, Philad[a] [7]

[2] His sister Amelia Jackson Holmes and his brother Edward Jackson Holmes were 18 and 15 years old respectively.

[3] The only poem found with Holmes's Civil War papers is reprinted immediately following this letter. There is, however, no direct evidence that this reference is to that poem.

[4] It is probable that this was Chauncey Wright, mathematician, philosopher, and friend of Holmes. Possibly, however, it was James Edward Wright, class secretary of the Class of 1861.

[5] Presumably Robert Pomeroy of Pittsfield. See, *infra*, p. 12.

[6] Charles Morris Walton of Philadelphia was for a brief time in Holmes's class at College. He was a cousin and intimate friend of Holmes's fellow officer and classmate Norwood Penrose Hallowell.

[7] Morris L. Hallowell was the father of Norwood Penrose Hallowell, *supra* note 6.

Lost and long-wandering at last I brake
From a deep forest's sullen-opening jaws,
Where hungry junipers stretched bony claws
Like traps of devils, baited with a snake—
And all around the dark rocks seemed to take
Forbidden shapes of things that man outlaws,
Speckled like toads, and patched with all the flaws
Of stormy days, and lichen-ringed, and black—
Then wearied out—"Is there no hope?" I cried—
Hearken—A soft melodious rapture thrills
As from the forest's deepest heart replied
Their hermit—and the music multiplied
And rose reechoing upward far and wide
From the dark valleys to the sunlit hills—

Camp Burnside[1]
Washington
Sept. 11, 1861

My Dear Mother

We are right in the midst of the work now—all sorts of camps around us—military discipline—and a regular soldier's life. We officers live on what we can get, buying milk, eggs, and lots of pies; (peach & apple price—12½) now getting meat & again not—On the whole we have had a very comfortable time however. Last night we pitched our tents here the most beautiful place we have been at either here or in Mass. Tomorrow morning we have marching orders again with one ration

[1] On September 10 the 20th Regiment had moved from Camp Kalorama to Camp Burnside on Meridian Hill about one mile from the Capitol.

in the haversacks. Destination will be known after we have started—We are under Gen. Lander[2] (a first rate man they say) in a Brigade with the 19th Mass & Burdan's sharp shooters[3] & a Co. of sharp shooters attached to our Reg't[4]—The Col.[5] is ranking Col. & it is said will be made Brig. General—this is not settled to my knowledge. Bartlett,[6] just come in, says we are to support Gen[l] Lander's HeadQr's on this side the River who asked for our Reg't (a big compliment)—This may be changed however.

In sight of where we are is the unfinished Capitol & from the neighboring Camp we hear the Bugle calls going all day.

[2] Brigadier General Frederick W. Lander at this time was commanding a brigade in General Stone's so-called Corps of Observation.

[3] Colonel Hiram Berdan's United States Sharpshooters.

[4] The 1st Company of Sharpshooters (Massachusetts), known as Andrew Sharpshooters, was commanded by Captain John Saunders.

[5] Colonel William Raymond Lee had commanded the 20th Regiment since its formation.

[6] Captain William Francis Bartlett, of the Harvard Class of 1862, at this time commanded Co. I in the 20th Regiment. He lost a leg at Yorktown in April, 1862, and later became Colonel of the 49th Regiment Massachusetts Volunteers, Colonel of the 57th Regiment Massachusetts Volunteers, and ultimately Brigadier General Commanding a Brigade in the Ninth Corps. After the publication of Francis W. Palfrey's *Memoir of William Francis Bartlett* (Boston, 1881), Holmes said of Bartlett:

"I knew him well; yet until that book I had not known the governing motive of his soul. I had admired him as a hero. When I read I learned to revere him as a saint. His strength was not in honor alone, but in religion, and those who do not share his creed must see that it was on the wings of religious faith that he mounted above even valiant deeds into an empyrean of ideal life."—Oliver Wendell Holmes, *Speeches* (Boston, 1934), p. 9.

Today we heard cannonading for 4 or 5 hrs & it is said there has been an engagement.—Now in comes Tremlett[7] & gives another story of our destination So I guess it's nowhither in particular. In the meanwhile I feel *very* well & in *very* good spirits and I think I am learning as I certainly am trying—I wish I could write details of our life but I am too impatient & have too little time to write long letters—However God bless you my darling I love you just as much as if I talked more with my mouth. God bless daddy too & love to the babbies I write again soon

Yours my dear
O. W. Holmes, Jr.

[Poolesville, Maryland]
September 23^d 1861.

My Dear Mother

This has been an eventful week to me as it has been the first that really looked like biz. Last Wednesday we (our company & Bartlett's) were suddenly ordered to fall in, pack up blankets & overcoats, received a number of rounds of cartridges and after a brief speech from Gen. Lander were sent marching off, we didn't know whither.[1] The General merely signified we had a post

[7] Captain Henry M. Tremlett, commanding Company A.

[1] On September 14 the 20th Regiment had moved from Camp Burnside to the neighborhood of Poolesville, Maryland. On the 15th they settled down at Camp Benton some two miles north of Edwards Ferry.

of honor & must do our duty. Well we first tramped off a couple of miles to Edward's Ferry and then across country—couldn't find the place—so back to ferry—Circumbendibus by night—arrive at last at an advanced battery of ours (Rhode Island) whence firing had taken place the day before—In silence we settle in a grove and lie down to pass the night as best may be—I had carried my invaluable carpet bag Whittier[2] his blankets which we shared—a drizzle & brief rain increased the liveliness of this first experience as groundlings (we had out our bedsteads on the march from Washington to where we now are, You remember.) But we were very tired & slept pretty well. Well, to cut it short, for, as usual, I irk the lengthened tale when told with pen—We stayed at the place till Saturday evening doing duty as an outpost near to the river, our pickets extending down to it & communicating with those of a Minnesota Reg. stationed along the banks of the Muddy Potomac. The first morning my eager eyes descry one man in a straw hat sitting unconcernedly on his tail apparently a guard on duty for the seceshers—Men & horses are seen from time to time from the tops of the trees and within cannon shot off to our right grows up from day to day an encampment with earthworks and what may be a heavy gun or so but of the last we are not sure—But firing

---

[2] Second Lieutenant Charles A. Whittier, Company A, later, as Major, A.D.C. to Major General John Sedgwick and to Major General Horatio G. Wright, successively commanding generals of the Sixth Corps.

across the river is forbidden so we sit & look & listen to their drums.

Of course proportionate distances are not Rept—the man in the straw hat is about ¾ or 1 mile from the top of our hill—the sharpshooters who were with us said they could plug him—but I doubt it. Edwards Ferry about 2 miles I guess from hill—To the rear of our hill & woods is a secesher's house where we eat & paid (.37) for delicious dinners of goose & ice-cream &c but the artillerymen hooked his pigs geese &c (for wh. their Lieut. commanding had to come down pretty well & got a reprimand to boot) This secesher has since been arrested for signalizing by lights from his house but evidence seems inconclusive & I guess he'll be released. The last night we were there we slept in

our boots & kept a horse saddled but though an attack
would have used us up I think we were about as safe in
their intentions as you were—Capt. Crowninshield's Co.
& that of Capt. Walleston[3] relieved us, unwilling to
leave goose & laziness, on Saturday evening—I had that
day a touch of diarrhea from drinking to [sic] much
milk on guard the night before—wh. soured on my
stomach & did not improve the results of wet & lying on
the ground without a blanket—an experiment you need
be at no fears of my repeating—I'm as well as ever now
though. Flour & water is an excellent & safe specific—
This was a mere touch & before & since I've been *very*
well—& weigh 136 lb. Last night (Sunday) or rather in
the afternoon about four o'cl'k we again bundled down
—this time the whole reg't except the aforesaid two
companies—to Edwards Ferry—there being news that
the Rebels had crossed—we slept in our clothes at the
Ferry all night—most of the officers at a buggy (bed—&
spider) house I in the middle of the road—Tremlett
leaving me in charge—I secured a convenient slant &
took a canteen for pillow but it was cold as the tenth
circle of Inferno—It seems wonderful though that I
mind the exposures little as I do—I get on as well as the
average of the men I should say—They were jumping
round at a great rate to get warm. I had a conviction
there'd be no trouble & there wasn't so at 5 A.M. this
morning home we pack again—All these things you see

[3] Captain Casper Crowninshield commanded Company D and Captain
Edmund A. Walleston commanded Company F.

give reality to the life but I don't expect any fighting for the present—

It seems so queer to see an encampment & twig men through a glass & think they are our enemies & hear of some of our pickets talking across & so on[4]—But I must get some sleep tonight—to make up for last & it gets late—I long for letters—write all of you all the time— The mails are irregular & the last I got was the one containing C. Walton's letter. You ask me if I like letters like yours. I delight in 'em. They are my great pleasure —Remember once for all that all details like those I've written of our actual or probable movements are strictly private as we are strongly forbidden to write about such things.

Love to everyone Bestest love to Dadkin also to A & N. Let them write Send Poem (& photog's) to Misses Pomeroy

Care Robert Pomeroy

Pittsfield, Mass.[5]

& then to C. Walton

Care M. L. Hallowell

Philad[a] Penn[a]

Goodnight my loveliest & sweetest

O. W. Holmes, Jr.

[4] Captain Bartlett, describing communications between the opposing pickets, has said that "in one case they exchanged a Boston Journal for a Mobile paper." Palfrey, *op. cit.* p. 11.

[5] In 1865 Agnes Pomeroy, daughter of Robert Pomeroy, leading citizen of Pittsfield, where Holmes spent many summers as a boy, was married to Brigadier General William Francis Bartlett. Her sister, Maria Center Pomeroy, later married Colonel Walter Cutting of New York.

STAFF OFFICERS, 20TH REGIMENT MASSACHUSETTS VOLUNTEERS

[20th Regiment Hospital, Camp Benton]
Wed: Oct. 23 1861

My Dear Mother

Here I am flat on my back after our first engagement —wounded but pretty comfortable[1]—I can't write an account now but I felt and acted very cool and did my duty I am sure—I was out in front of our men encouraging 'em on when a spent shot knocked the wind out of me & I fell—then I crawled to the rear a few paces & rose by help of the 1st Ser^gt;[2] & the Colonel who was passing said "That's right Mr Holmes—Go to the Rear" but I felt that I couldn't without more excuse so up I got and rushed to the front where hearing the Col. cheering the men on I waved my sword and asked if none would follow me when down I went again by the Colonel's side—The first shot (the spent ball) struck me on the belly below where the ribs separate & bruised & knocked the wind out of me—The second time I hope only one ball struck me entering the left & coming out behind the right breast in wh. case I shall probably recover and this view is seconded by finding a ball in my clothes by the right hand wound—I may be hit twice in which case the chance is not so good—But I am now so well that I have good hopes—The first night I made up

[1] On October 21 a small Union force, including units of the 20th Regiment crossed the Potomac at Harrison's Island, and were engaged in a brief and unsuccessful engagement with the Confederate forces at Ball's Bluff on the Virginia shore.

[2] Henry J. Smith, First Sergeant, Company A.

Wdt: Oct. 23 1861

My Dear Mother

Here I am flat
on my back after our first
engagement — wounded but pretty
comfortable — I can't write an
account now but I felt and acted
very cool and did my duty. I am sure —
I was out in front of our men encouraging
'em on when a spent shot knocked
the wind out of me — & I fell. Then
I crawled to the rear a few paces & rose by
help of the 1st Sergt; & the Colonel who was
passing said "Pretty right Mr Holmes — Go to the
Rear" but I felt that I couldn't
without more excuse so up I got
and rushed to the front where
hearing the Col. cheering the

men on I waved my sword
and asked if young would
follow me where

by the right hand wound -
I may be hit twice
in which case the
chance is not so good.
But I am now so well
that I have good hopes -
The first night I made
up my mind to die &
was going to take that
little bottle of laudanum
as soon as I was sure
of dying with any
pain - but the doctors
told me not to take it.
And now seem to think
I have a fair chance
God bless you

whatever happens in the conviction that my dear friend Keppel is very

my mind to die & was going to take that little bottle of laudanum as soon as I was sure of dying with any pain—but the doctors told me not to take it. And now seem to think I have a fair chance and all my friends whatever happens I am very happy in the conviction I did my duty handsomely—Lt Putnam is dead[3] Capt. Putnam[4] lost his right arm. Hallowell[5] fought like a brick but wasn't hurt—Schmidt[6] badly wounded—Lowell wounded[7]—Colonel Major & Adjutant probably prisoners Babo & Wesselhoeft probably dead[8]—Dreher[9] shot through the head—Serg^t Merchant shot dead (in the head)[10] From a third to a half of our company killed wounded & prisoners

I have written a few details if you can read 'em[11]—Men are concentrating in all directions and fighting still going on—They begun by cutting up the 20th only 8 officers out of 22 in our Regt got home unhurt I hope

[3] Second Lieutenant William Lowell Putnam, Company E.

[4] Captain John C. Putnam, Company H.

[5] First Lieutenant Norwood Penrose Hallowell, Company H.

[6] Captain George A. Schmitt, Company E, had been Holmes's instructor in German at Harvard College.

[7] First Lieutenant James Jackson Lowell, Company E, died on July 6, 1862, as a result of wounds received at the battle of Glendale.

[8] Captain Alvis Babo, Company G, and Second Lieutenant Reinhold Wesselhoeft, Company C, were drowned while swimming to Harrison's Island after the engagement at Ball's Bluff.

[9] Captain Ferdinand Dreher, Company C.

[10] John Merchant, Sergeant, Company A.

[11] This memorandum does not appear to have been preserved.

we'll lick 'em yet though—I was hit in the beginning of the fight,

Yours Always
O W Holmes Jr

God bless you

I can't send a good looking note lying on my back—But I believe Whit. has written you[12]

---

[12] A long letter, dated October 22, from Lieutenant Whittier to Dr. Holmes describing the battle of Ball's Bluff has been preserved.

DIARY, BALL'S BLUFF

[DIARY]

No. 2.[1]

There are a great many things of course,—thoughts, occupations & events,—of which I wish I'd kept Memoranda during my past life—But I wish especially that after the military affairs—battles etc. in which I've been concerned I had noted many of those facts which so rapidly escape the memory in the mist which settles over a fought field.

Wound at Ball's Bluff

Not to speak of while the fight was actually going on, I have been struck with the intensity of the mind's action and its increased suggestiveness, after one has received a wound—

At Ball's Bluff, Tremlett's boy George told me, I was hit at 4½ P.M., *the heavy firing having begun about an hour before, by the watch*—I felt as if a horse had kicked me and went over—1st Serg^t Smith grabbed me and lugged me to the rear a little way & opened my shirt and ecce! the [the] two holes in my breasts & the bullet, which he gave me—George says he squeezed it from the right opening—Well—I remember the sickening feeling

[1] The significance of this number is not known. This account of Holmes's wounding at Ball's Bluff was apparently written by him some time after the event but while he was on active duty. It was found on loose sheets in the small diary which he kept from May to July, 1864. It seems not improbable that the pages formed a special section in the earlier diary which has disappeared. Apparently the pages were removed from that diary with some care and intentionally preserved.

of water in my face—I was quite faint—and seeing poor Serg^t Merchant lying near—shot through the head and covered with blood—and then the thinking begun— (Meanwhile hardly able to speak—at least, coherently) —Shot through the lungs? Lets see—and I spit—Yes— already the blood was in my mouth. At once my thoughts jumped to "Children of the New Forest." (by Marryatt) which I was fond of reading as a little boy, and in which the father of one of the heroines is shot through the lungs by a robber—I remembered he died with terrible haemorrhages & great agony—What should I do? Just then I remembered and felt in my waist coat pocket—Yes there it was—a little bottle of laudanum which I had brought along—But I won't take it yet; no, see a doctor first—It may not be as bad as it looks—At any rate wait till the pain begins—

When I had got to the bottom of the Bluff the ferry boat, (the scow,) had just started with a load—but there was a small boat there—Then, still in this half conscious state, I heard somebody groan—Then I thought "Now wouldn't Sir Philip Sydney have that other feller put into the boat first?" But the question, as the form in which it occurred shows, came from a *mind* still bent on a becoming and consistent carrying out of its ideals of conduct—not from the unhesitating instinct of a still predominant & heroic *will*—I am not sure whether I propounded the question but I let myself be put aboard.

I never have been able to account for the fact that

bullets struck in the bank of the island over our heads as we were crossing—Well; the next question was how to get me from the ferry to the hospital—this I solved by another early recollection—the "Armchair"—Two men crossed their hands in such a way that I could sit on 'em & put my arms round their necks—& so they carried me —The little house was filled so I was taken into the large building which served as a general hospital; and I remember the coup d'oeuil on which I closed my eyes with the same sickening which I had felt on seeing poor Merchant—Men lying round on the floor—the spectacle wasn't familiar then—a red blanket with an arm lying on it in a pool of blood—it seems as if instinct told me it was John Putnam's (then Capt. Comdg Co H)— and near the entrance a surgeon calmly grasping a man's finger and cutting it off—both standing—while the victim contemplated the operation with a very grievous mug. Well presently old Hayward [2] approached and inspected me—"How does it look, Doctor, shall I recover? Tell me the truth for I really want to know"—(It seemed then and does now as if I was perfectly rational but Whittier says that when he saw me later I was very light headed—) Hayward in his deliberate way— "We-ell, you *may* recover—Gen. Shields did" [3]— Shields! I'd thought of him before and got small com-

[2] Nathan Hayward, Surgeon of the 20th Regiment.
[3] Major General James Shields in the battle of Cerro Gordo in the Mexican War had been hit by a grapeshot which entered his chest, passed through his lung, and came out near his spine. The wound was treated by drawing a silk handkerchief through it on a ramrod.

fort from that—we all thought that night that I had a couple of bullets in my lungs—& I bled from them (at the mouth) very freely—"That means the chances are against me, don't it?" "Ye-es, the chances are against you"—Meanwhile he picked something from the left opening—I thought it was bone till he told me it was a bit of flannel—again I felt for the laudanum and again determined to wait till pain or sinking strength warned me of the end being near—I didn't feel sure there was no chance—and watching myself did not feel the hand of death upon me beyond a hope—my strength seemed to hold out too well.

After this my recollection of events is confused—I remember poor Willy Putnam's groans—and his refusing to let the Dr. operate on him, saying he knew the wound was mortal and it would only be more pain for nothing—I remember hobnobbing with the man who lay near me, and when to my astonishment John O'Sullivan (Whit's & my serv[t]) appeared telling him to help my neighbor too, and feeling very heroic after that speech—(By the way Hayward had turned me on my breast & this may have helped a good deal of the wound to heal almost by first intention)—I remember being very sleepy—(some enlisted man has since told me he gave me some coffee and my face flushed and I went right off—) & presently a Doctor of (Baxter's?) Fire Zouaves[4] coming in with much noise & bluster, and

[4] The 72nd Regiment Pennsylvania Volunteers, under Colonel DeWitt Clinton Baxter, was commonly known as Baxter's Fire Zouaves.

oh, troops were crossing to the Virginia side, and we were going to lick, and Heaven knows what not—I called him and gave him my address and told him (or meant & tried to) if I died to write home & tell 'em I'd done my duty—I was very anxious they should know that—and I then imparted to him my laudanum scheme —This he dissuaded and gave me a dose of some opiate —he said it wasn't laudanum, but I guess that was a white lie—and when I slumbered I believe he prigged the bottle—

Pen[5] before I was moved came in & kissed me and went away again—Whittier came & saw me too, though I'm not sure if I remember it—and Sturgis[6] of whom anon—I think I remember the confusion when some bullets struck the house—and the story that the enemy would shell the island. But all these recollections are obscure and the order of their occurrence uncertain—

Much more vivid is my memory of my thoughts and state of mind for though I may have been light-headed my reason was working—even if through a cloud. Of course when I thought I was dying the reflection that the majority vote of the civilized world declared that with my opinions I was *en route* for Hell came up with painful distinctness—Perhaps the first impulse was tremulous—but then I said—by Jove, I die like a soldier anyhow—I was shot in the breast doing my duty up to the hub—afraid? No, I am proud—then I thought I

[5] First Lieutenant Norwood Penrose Hallowell.
[6] Second Lieutenant Henry H. Sturgis, Company H.

couldn't be guilty of a deathbed recantation—father and I had talked of that and were agreed that it generally meant nothing but a cowardly giving way to fear —Besides, thought I, can I recant if I want to, has the approach of death changed my beliefs much? & to this I answered—No—Then came in my Philosophy—I am to take a leap in the dark—but now as ever I believe that whatever shall happen is best—for it is in accordance with a general law—and *good* & *universal* (or *general law*) are synonymous terms in the universe—(I can now add that our phrase *good* only means certain general truths seen through the heart & will instead of being merely contemplated intellectually—I doubt if the intellect accepts or recognizes that classification of good and bad). Would the complex forces which made a still more complex unit in *Me* resolve themselves back into simpler forms or would my angel be still winging his way onward when eternities had passed? I could not tell—But all was doubtless well—and so with a "God forgive me if I'm wrong" I slept—But while I was debating with myself Harry Sturgis bulged upon the scene —I don't remember what I said—I know what I wanted —it was the cool opinion of an outsider—a looker-on— as a *point d'appui* for resistance or a που στω from which to spring aloft, as the case might be; at any rate a foreign substance round which my thoughts could crystallize— Sturge I hear says I was very profane, to this effect— "Well Harry I'm dying but I'll be G. d'd if I know where I'm going"—But I doubt it although a little later

I swore frightfully—to the great horror of John O'S. who tried to stop me thinking I was booking myself for Hell rapidly. Sturge thereat with about his usual tact, begun "Why—Homey—you believe in Christ, don't you" etc. with a brief exposition of doctrine argumentatively set forth—I gave him my love for Pen whom I'd not yet seen, & the same message home which I subsequently gave the Fire Zouave Surgeon and Sturge departed—Later I only can recall, in a general way, being carried across the Island in a blanket—lying on the bank comatose, being ferried across to the M^d shore with some hitch (we came mighty near being upset I heard afterwards)—swearing terrifically as I've said—and finally after being put in the hold of a canal boat and the hatches or scuttle or whatever you call it tumbling in and nearly all but smashing me & one or two others into sudden death, that I muzzed away the time till we got to Edwards Ferry—

N.B. I forgot to mention on the second page of this account, that I believe it was while I was being taken down the Bluff—that I said to myself in rather grim pleasantry—"Whittier Brevet First Lieutenant"—

I was taken from the Canal boat and put into one of the two wheeled ambulances which were then in vogue as one form of torture—Captain Dreher was my companion—shot through the head & insensible, but breathing heavily—The Ambulance was broken—the horse baulked and the man didn't know how to drive—whenever we came to a hill, & there were several, there we stopped, head downward, till some of the men along the road gave us a boost & started our horse forward again— I suffered much in mind—for what with the rough riding & my momentary expectations of being upset I hardly thought to reach camp alive—There was a piece of road which Sturge had built & on which he prided himself not a little; my aching bones told me when we reached that Via Mala—Fortunately I directed our driver to go to the Regt. instead of to Poolesville and we got to the Hospital at early dawn—There were many commiserating exclamations—Hibbard [7] (then pr. H. Co. A.) who was there, sick, insisted on turning out and giving me his bed—Then for the first time I saw Dreher—a ghastly spectacle—Two black cavities seemed all that there was left for eyes—his whiskers & beard matted with blood which still poured black, from his mouth—and a most horrible stench—

The Hospital Steward—a cockeyed Dutchman who afterwards stuck me certain shekels for his services— looked at my wound and conjectured the true state of affairs—bound me round with an infernal bandage (which Hayward cut as soon as he saw,) having first rammed plugs of lint into the holes, and then left me uncomfortable but still exceedingly joyful, for he had told me I should live—I could have hugged him for that—After this—whiskey—lightheadedness—laudanum & a request (the old idea still haunting me) to Peter

[7] Private Lansing E. Hibbard was commissioned Second Lieutenant November 12, 1862.

Wilkins[8] to get me a quart of laudanum—which, he has told me, he did, more or less—Peter like!

I remember Hayward's saying "It is a beautiful face." or something of the sort & looking up & seeing Willy Putnam, calm & lovely, and being told or knowing he was dead—I was soon moved to a Wall Tent with John Putnam where all was quiet (Tremlett here astonished me with his tenderness & even Wollaston[9] when he returned from Boston had tears in his eyes as he looked on John). Maj. Gen. Banks[10] came in (see his letter home)[11] Gordon[12] & Andrews[13] of the 2nd—Mr. Hovey[14] etc. and things went smoothly barring my impatience till I started for Phila with Bill Hallowell[15]— memorable time when my temper gained me his lasting dislikes—He was only too kind to me—

Notes to account of my first wound

1. At first I only intended to show the rapidity of thought & queer suggestions which occur when one is

[8] Presumably Henry E. Wilkins, who was to be commissioned First Lieutenant in the 20th Regiment on January 6, 1862. See Dr. Holmes, *My Hunt After "The Captain"* (Riverside Lit. Series, No. 31, 1911), p. 20.

[9] Presumably Captain Edmund A. Walleston.

[10] Major General Nathaniel P. Banks of Massachusetts was Divisional Commander under General McClellan.

[11] This letter, dated October 25, describing the General's glimpse of Holmes on the previous day, has been preserved.

[12] George H. Gordon, then Colonel, commanding the 2nd Regiment Massachusetts Volunteers.

[13] Lieutenant Colonel George L. Andrews.

[14] Not identified.

[15] Presumably William Penrose Hallowell, brother of Norwood P. Hallowell, and at this time a civilian.

hit, but as I always wanted to have a memorandum of this experience—so novel at that time to all & especially so to me from the novelty of the service and my youth—I have told the whole story from time I was hit until apprehension had left me—

2. I must add one more confession. While I was lying on the island, one of the thoughts that made it seem particularly hard to die was the recollection of several fair damsels whom I wasn't quite ready to leave—

3. Charley Pearson[16] told me when I saw him in Washington after my wound at the 2nd Fredericksburg, that a gentleman told him that visiting Harrison's Island and looking round for a relic he came on a bloodstained handkerchief marked "Lt. O W Holmes, Jr." "20th Regt. Mass. Vols." which he pouched & preserved—[17]

4. It is curious how rapidly the mind adjusts itself under some circumstances to entirely new relations—I thought for awhile that I was dying, and it seemed the most natural thing in the world—The moment the hope of life returned it seemed as abhorrent to nature as ever that I should die—

5. Curious time on arriving at Georgetown by canal—Bill H. got a ramshackle vehicle—one horse & negro

[16] First Lieutenant Charles L. Peirson, Adjutant of the 20th Regiment, was captured at Ball's Bluff with Colonel Lee and other staff officers, later served on the staffs of Generals N. J. T. Dana and John Sedgwick, and in August, 1862, was made Lieutenant Colonel in the 39th Regiment Massachusetts Volunteers.

[17] The handkerchief was eventually returned to Holmes and has been preserved.

driver which both went to sleep whenever we stopped —I, my trunk & John O'S. in rear part—On getting to the White House I wanted to see it & our equipage boldly drove in & by the door—We had the greatest difficulty in finding a place at any Hotel—Willard's full but an officer offered his room which of course I didn't take—"Mr. Brown" (*Metropolitan* now, then called Secesh) "says he *won't* have him"—another says yes but finding he'd mistaken the man backs out—finally at the National we were kindly entreated—[18]

[18] Following this long passage headed "No. 2" there is a list of the officers and men of the 20th who were killed or wounded at Ball's Bluff, Yorktown, Seven Days, Antietam, First Fredericksburg, Second Fredericksburg (Chancellorsville), and Gettysburg. The list concludes with an entry that after Gettysburg Captain Thomas M. McKay was murdered by a deserter. The murder occurred on October 6, 1863. This whole list of casualties bears the heading "No. 3."

LETTERS, MARCH 1862—DECEMBER 1862

Tuesday Ev'g—
Mar. [25] 1862[1]

My Dear Parents—

I stopped 24 hr's at Phil'd[a] and met Tremlett in the cars this morn'g—We arrived this evn'g at Washington & just as the cars stopped beheld the 20th only then arrived—I shall report for duty tomorrow but stop tonight at the National preferring even a bad hostelry to a promiscuous barn—Don't like the looks of things under Palf. wish Lee was here[2]—We are in Dana's brigade (good man) Sedgwick's Division & Sumner's Corps d'Armee or vice versa—I forget which[3]—I am in good spirits & things look natural & easy—I'm just returned fr. a supper with the officers of the 20th—I have left my trunk at Phil[a] where it will remain for the present—sub-

[1] Holmes had been on leave in Boston since his wounding at Ball's Bluff. For a part of the time he had apparently been on recruiting duty in Boston and Pittsfield. (See J. T. Morse, Jr., *Life and Letters of Oliver Wendell Holmes* (Boston, 1896), II, 163; Carolyn Kellogg Cushing, "The Gallant Captain and the Little Girl," *Atlantic Monthly*, CLV (May, 1935), 545.) The 20th had remained at Camp Benton (Poolesville) until February 26, 1862, and had, after several moves, left Bolivar Heights near Harper's Ferry, on March 24, for Washington. It is unlikely that they arrived there before the 25th. See *Annual Report of the Adjutant-General (Massachusetts) for 1862* (Boston, 1863), 229; George A. Bruce, *The Twentieth Regiment of Massachusetts Volunteer Infantry, 1861-1865* (Boston, 1906), p. 80; and *History of the Nineteenth Regiment Massachusetts Volunteer Infantry, 1861-1865* (Salem, 1906), p. 54.

[2] Colonel William Raymond Lee had been taken prisoner at Ball's Bluff. During his absence Lieutenant Colonel Francis W. Palfrey commanded the Regiment.

[3] The 20th Regiment was in the 3rd Brigade (Brigadier General N. J. T. Dana commanding) of Brigadier General John Sedgwick's Division in the Second Corps commanded by Major General Edwin V. Sumner.

ject to my order—Officers have reduced baggage to a very few portables—Nobody knows—but we may go on a naval expedition—

Whatever happens Keep up your pluck

Love to all from yours affectionately

O. W. Holmes, Jr.

Tuesday April 7. 1861. [*sic*]¹
or Wednesday 1 A.M. rather—
((unless I am a day behind time—))

My Dear Parents—

I am on guard tonight and seize the chance to write —John Put. goes to the fort tomorrow and will take my letter²—We are on the advance with about 130 000 men & George B.³ in person—Our division is the center & at present I believe he remains with us—I have seen him twice—It's a campaign now & no mistake—No tents, no trunks—no nothing—it has rained like the devil last

---

¹ The 20th Regiment boarded the transport "Catskill" on March 27, and sailed from Washington on the 28th, arriving at Hampton, Virginia, on March 31, 1862. The Regiment went into bivouac for the night one mile outside of Hampton on the road to Big Bethel. In the next days the Union forces advanced up the Peninsula and, on the night of the 6th, the 20th camped four miles beyond Big Bethel and within some five miles of Yorktown.

² Captain Bartlett on April 10, 1862, wrote to his mother: "John Putnam is going back to Fort Monroe; he can't stand this, it is too rough for him." Palfrey, *op. cit.* p. 38.

³ On March 11 General McClellan, having been removed as General-in-Chief, had assumed command of the Army of the Potomac.

night all day and tonight and you may guess what the mud is in a clayey soil where it was a real annoyance before—Marching will have to be slow for the roads have constantly to be made or mended for artillery (of wh. there is a great deal) The men and officers are wet enough you may believe but there is real pluck shown now as these are real hardships to contend with. But yesterday (i.e. Monday unless all my days are one behindhand) it was cold comfort to come back to a camping ground with which the Boston Common parade ground at its worst offers a favorable contrast after a march up to knees in mud all day on a reconnoisance on wh. our Brigade was sent. We are in camp within 4 miles of the enemie's fortifications & approached to within ½ a mile—There was firing (with one piece of artillery with shell from the rebs none on our side—) all day—volleys & scattering shots from the enemy returned by the 19th & Jack Saunder's Sharp Shooters— We knew biz. wasn't intended as we went out for Lt ? Comstock of the engineers[4] to make drawings—But late in the afternoon after several changes of position on our part we drew into a field on the other side of wh. was an earthwork & aforesaid gun—our posit. was concealed by rising ground or a shell w'ld have blown some of us to pieces—They kept firing into the edge of the woods where the 19th were deployed as skirmishers & succeeded in killing one & wounding 1 or 2. as we were

[4] Lieutenant C. B. Comstock was actively engaged in reconnaissance of the terrain throughout the Peninsula Campaign.

in line of battle had they known our whereabouts it w'ld have been bad.

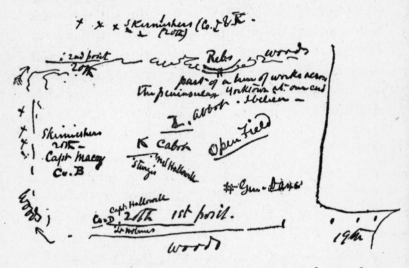

When we saw Co I (Lt. Abbot[5]—) go forward up the hill I fairly trembled for though they marched with

[5] First Lieutenant Henry L. Abbott, later Major commanding the 20th Regiment, was among Holmes's most intimate friends in the Regiment. The son of Judge Josiah G. Abbott of Lowell, Massachusetts, he had been graduated from Harvard College in 1860 and enlisted in the 4th Battalion and gone to Fort Independence with Holmes in April, 1861. He was undoubtedly the most distinguished soldier in the 20th Regiment. After surviving all the earlier battles of the Regiment he was killed in the Wilderness Campaign on May 6, 1864. To his friends he was known as "Little" Abbott. His older brother and college classmate, Captain Edward Gardner Abbott of the 2nd Regiment Massachusetts Volunteers, was killed at Cedar Mountain, August 9, 1862. In Holmes's Memorial Day Address, delivered on May 30, 1884, he spoke of Henry L. Abbott as follows:

"There is one who on this day is always present to my mind. He entered the army at nineteen, a second lieutenant. In the Wilderness, already at the head of his regiment, he fell, using the moment that was

splendid coolness I expected to see some bowled over every minute—but just as they were in sight of the works Comstock & Bartlett (who is much better than Palf. who isn't worth a ——) ran forward and ordered Abbot (who had misunderstood the order) under cover as skirmishers—then Cabots Co. K[6]—(Ned Hallowell, 2nd Lt.)[7] went forward & then the battalion marched by the left flank to posit. no 2. by the edge of the woods Then the skirmishers fired a little or were

---

left him of life to give all his little fortune to his soldiers. I saw him in camp, on the march, in action. I crossed debatable land with him when we were rejoining the army together. I observed him in every kind of duty, and never in all the time that I knew him did I see him fail to choose that alternative of conduct which was most disagreeable to himself. He was indeed a Puritan in all his virtues, without the Puritan austerity; for, when duty was at an end, he who had been the master and leader became the chosen companion in every pleasure that a man might honestly enjoy. In action he was sublime. His few surviving companions will never forget the awful spectacle of his advance alone with his company in the streets of Fredericksburg. In less than sixty seconds he would become the focus of a hidden and annihilating fire from a semicircle of houses. His first platoon had vanished under it in an instant, ten men falling dead by his side. He had quietly turned back to where the other half of his company was waiting, had given the order, "Second platoon, forward!" and was again moving on, in obedience to superior command, to certain and useless death, when the order he was obeying was countermanded. The end was distant only a few seconds; but if you had seen him with his indifferent carriage, and sword swinging from his finger like a cane, you never would have suspected that he was doing more than conducting a company drill on the camp parade ground. He was little more than a boy, but the grizzled corps commanders knew and admired him; and for us, who not only admired, but loved, his death seemed to end a portion of our life also."—Holmes, *op. cit. supra*, pp. 7-8.

[6] Captain Charles F. Cabot, killed at Fredericksburg, December 11, 1862.

[7] Second Lieutenant Edward N. Hallowell was the brother of Captain Norwood Penrose Hallowell.

fired at rather—and then having found out all we wanted to know we turned round & marched home—well tired out—I am in good spirits though of course I despise the life in itself outside of special circumstances & principles—If I can stand this very rough beginning it will be good for my health I am in Pen's Co.[8] and it makes all the difference in the world—that is an un-mixed pleasure—I caught a heavy cold on board the boat—& I have still something of a cough a *fact* wh. annoys me though the thing itself doesn't—I think I shall stand the work—You must write *all the time* though I can but rarely with great uncertainty whether my letter goes—acknowledge the receipt of mine and be constant in writing even if you don't hear for a long time as they have a way of stopping the mails here & at any rate I rarely can—Anything you want to show any of my friends (wh. isn't private that is) you may for I can't write although I long to hear—

> God bless you all
> O. W. Holmes, Jr.

My hand is cold so that I sling a nasty quill—

[8] Company D, under Captain Hallowell.

April 17, 1862[1]

From the Woods near the enemy

Dear Mother

I am very well & in fine spirits, gaining flesh—We are in the reserve—a compliment—(best troops) I write just a word as I have a chance by a discharged man going home. Give my love to all & tell 'em to write— If there should be a fight we are ready & eager—Don't give y'rself causeless uneasiness untill you hear of one— however—nor then either—My dearest love to Dad & y'rself—

O W Holmes Jr.

April 23. 1862

My Dear Parents

We are still in the same spot from wh. I wrote a hurried note by a discharged man who promised to deliver it and also a business letter concerning pay for Recr^s Service wh. I hope you rec^d [1]—Did you? The latter I sent by mail—We go on picket every third day and it would have made you smile to see Pen and me

---

[1] From April 7 to April 16 the Regiment had remained at Camp Winfield Scott in the neighborhood of Wynn's Mill some three miles south of Yorktown. Following the abortive crossing and re-crossing of Warwick Creek by the left flank on April 16, General McClellan concentrated all efforts upon preparations for a direct assault on the fortifications at Yorktown.

[1] The business letter referred to has not been located.

yesterday morn'g sitting on a stump smoking our pipes
& reading old letters after a night of raining like blazes,
out in the woods with a constant popping of guns where
the reb⁸ and our men were exchanging compliments &
every now & then *bang—boom*—as a shell was fired &
exploded on the one side or t'other—we fire most—
Now and then a bullet would whiz high over our heads
from the other side.

Our pickets are pushed out to the edge of a marsh on
the other side of wh. the reb⁸ have their earthworks &
wh. they can drain when they desire, by means of a
water gate—We go on again tomorrow—

The notion now seems to be that McClellan is trying
to out-general & catch 'em if poss. without a big fight—
Tell Amelia I was delighted with her letter and if I don't
answer it—it is want of time & opportunity. My dear
A. knows I always delighted in her letters and I want
her to write often—once a week is seldom—I tell you
you can't realize how we long to hear from home out
here and other fellows The Hˢ ² for instance get at least
one & generally more letters every mail (i.e. two days)
while I hardly get one a week—My cold seems to have
finally departed and except that the two rainy days
before & while on picket my bowels played the Devil
with me owing to cold & wet and want of sleep I have
been very well

Today I'm all right again except the clearing up

---

² Presumably Captain and Lieutenant Hallowell.

rumbles of the storm. In short all is exceedingly well except the fewness of letters & diminishing chance of a fight. Pittsburgh Landing seems to have been rather an equivocal victory after all[3]—by the way—Doesn't it? Have you given my messages about writing?

Capt. Hallowell & Lt. Holmes (qui hoc fecit) as they appeared poking their smipes under my india rubber while on picket during the rain—Observe I have cut down the stem of the meerschaum making it much more nobby—N. P. H. smokes a clay—

Weight of O W H. Jr in uniform & without any impediment 144 lbs! some time ago—

As I've said, I shan't accept the Captaincy[4] (if it's true—the official notice hasn't yet come). It was done without Palf.'s knowledge wh. I don't approve of—however little of a soldier he may be —&

[3] The Battle of Shiloh (Pittsburgh Landing) had come to a close on April 7, with the repulse of the Confederates, who had sought to cut off Grant's forces from the Tennessee River. General Grant failed to develop the advantages which he had secured on the 7th in the recovery of all positions lost on the previous day.

[4] Holmes was commissioned Captain by Governor Andrew by order dated March 23, 1862. In the Peninsula Campaign he commanded Company G.

he isn't much—Bartlett does all the work—Besides
I'm much more contented & happy as I am—You
needn't say this—as I want to receive the off. notice
seeing it's been in the paper—

Love to Amelia & Ned—Tell people to write—
Most affectionately
Your son
O. W. Holmes, Jr.

I forgot to say that as our camp is only about ½ mile
from the pickets in a bee line—we are called under arms
about every third night by some infernal Reg^t or other
getting excited & banging away for about 5 minutes—
We stand about an hour in the mud & then are dis-
missed—"Men will keep on equipments ready to fall in
at a moments notice"—Com^y improves Penn h'd'k'fs are
in my trunk at Phil^a

25th April 1862

Dear Mother

Rec'd today yr's of Easter Sunday—Thank you
much for it—The mail is just going & I only write to say
all well & God bless you dearest—The Reg^t has suffered
a gr't loss by Capt. Bartlett's being shot in left leg yester-

day wh. is amputated just above the knee—he bore it bravely—He was hit at one of the posts on picket—

Love to all—

Afftly

O. W. H., Jr.

Rec'd today also—one fr. F. McG.[1] 1 fr. F. D.[2] &

" " I. Agassiz[3]—Rec'd. $3 &

stamps

O. W. H., Jr.

Written on field of battle—

June 2nd '62[1]

Dear Parents

I am nearly tired out with the constant labors of the last two days but I write a word to say I with all our officers am safe so far and I am in perfect health & spirits[2]—

[1] Presumably Miss Fanny McGregor.

[2] Presumably Fanny Bowditch Dixwell, whom Holmes married in 1872.

[3] Ida Agassiz, daughter of Professor Louis Agassiz, married Major Henry Lee Higginson in December, 1863.

---

[1] On the back of the envelope was written: "Send a toothbrush in a big envelope."

[2] On May 4 the 20th Regiment had entered Yorktown after its evacuation by the Confederates. The Regiment did not participate in the Williamsburg campaign but on May 6 was moved by water from Yorktown to a point on the Pamunkey River above West Point. From that time until May 31 it moved up and across the Peninsula, passing through or near Eltham Landing, Cumberland Landing, New Kent Court House, Baltimore Crossroads, and Bottom's Bridge. On May 28 the Regiment,

May 31ˢᵗ We heard heavy firing from Casey's Divⁿ [3] and soon our Div was under arms & marched 4 miles I sh'ld think—the last part through a stream above our knees and then double quick through mud a foot deep on to the field of battle

at the place marked *1ˢᵗ line* we were at once drawn up

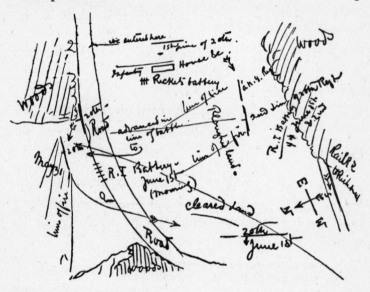

partly covered by the house & the land rising fr. us to the house—At this time Rickets Battery[4] was firing hard

---

still part of Dana's Brigade, encamped on the north bank of the Chickahominy near the Tyler House. It was from this position that the 20th moved forward on the 31st into the Battle of Fair Oaks. It crossed the Chickahominy by the Grapevine Bridge. See map of Fair Oaks, *infra*, p. 89.

[3] Brigadier General Silas Casey, commanding the 3rd Division in the Fourth Corps.

[4] Battery I of Ricketts' First United States Battery was commanded by Brigadier General Edmund Kirby.

and sheets of flame came fr. the line of Inft[y] as a couple of Co[s], only, (they say) of the Reb[s] tried to charge the guns. They were mowed down and broke—The shingles of the house rattled with the hail of Reb. bullets and many whistled by—mostly over us wounding one or two—Here I saw an officer just in front of our line lying snug behind a stump apparently, too, unhurt— Soon we filed round and *formed under* fire in 2nd posit. left of a N. Y. Regt.[5] and opened fire on the Reb. Line wh. was visible—Our fire was soon stopped (by order) and we could see in the field, (where our 3[d] posit. was later,) Reb[s] moving by twos & threes—apparently broken up—Then the order was given Forward in line —Double quick—At this point thinking there must be a battery nearer than I thought to be charged—I threw away my haversack wh. impeded my motions containing all my food my dressing case my only change of stockings my pipe & tobacco—wh. I have vainly lamented since—(The land was soft fr. ploughing wh. made it hard to get on) When we got to the road the R. wing entered the woods firing hard and the left wing (I am next the colors on the left of the color Co.—Hallowells place, as 9th Capt., but wh. I keep as the previous posit. of Co G. on acc't of the smallness of Co D.) the left wing advancing more slowly to avoid getting fired into by our own men—A Co. of Reb[s] trying to pass out of the woods was knocked to pieces—and thus we soon took the final posit. of the 1st day marked—((Here I

[5] 34th Regiment New York Volunteers.

was interrupted by firing near at hand—It turns out to be Reb^s firing at a party of our men who are burying *their dead!*))—marked May 31—Here we blazed away left oblique into the woods till we were ordered to cease firing & remained masters of the field (we were the only Reg^t there) where the enemy had just been—Then the bringing in of the wounded begun—Among them were the Brig. Genl Pettigrew I think of the Hampton Legion S. C. (wh. is among their best troops—as indeed were all the Rebs—engaged—) a Lt. Col. &c. We sat under arms waiting sleepless cold wet and hungry till morng for the renewal of the fight—June 1st there was heavy firing from 7 am. till noon in the woods along the R.R. and we were formed at the place marked June 1st about wh. we have since continued—We are now shoved forward a hundred or two feet to the woods—June 1st nothing particular occurred—We stayed in line all day—formed sq. to resist an expected attack of cavalry in the afternoon—OWH in the front rank of 1st front handling a sword & pistol—and were fired at several times during the day by sharp shooters—A bullet has a most villainous greasy slide through the air—In the night Co^s D, C, & G on picket in woods in front of Regt. up again nearly all night. Thunder wind & rain—Our men fired at once by Reb^s & a shell dropped among us from our own side—We heard the Reb^s working talking & knocking round all night and this morn'g it seems they have fallen back a little—

Today is pleasant and hot—It is singular with what indifference one gets to look on the dead bodies in gray clothes wh. lie all around—(or rather did—We are burying them today as fast as we can—) As you go through the woods you stumble constantly, and, if after dark, as last night on picket, perhaps tread on the swollen bodies already fly blown and decaying, of men shot in the head back or bowels—Many of the wounds are terrible to look at—especially those fr. fragments of shell, Co G although roughs & poor material fought splendidly especially after the first flurry when they had settled down to the work—Once when *entre nous* the right of Lowell's Co begun to waver a little and fall back our left stood and didn't give an inch—But really as much or rather more is due to the file closers than anything else I told 'em to shoot any man who ran and they lustily buffeted every hesitating brother—I gave one (who was cowering) a smart rap over the backsides with the edge of my sword—and stood with my revolver & swore I'd shoot the first who ran or fired against orders —Well we licked 'em and this time there was the maneuvering of a battle to be seen—splendid and awful to behold; especially as the dusk allowed us to see clearly the lines of flames from the different Regt[s] as they fired—

We have had so far I fancy about fr. 20 to 25 killed & wounded in our Regt*—No officers though Pen had a bullet cut the rubber blanket he had round him sack

* 400 fighting men strong perhaps

fashion across the breast. Among our prisoners were men fr. Vᵃ N.C.; S.C.; Gᵃ/ Alᵃ/ Miss./ Lᵃ/ Texas/ Tennessee I doubt if we fight more at present but we are in spirits though worn by fatigue and privation as well as mental anxiety—

If I am killed you will find a Mem. on the back of a picture I carry wh. please attend to. I must sleep a few minutes I can hardly keep my eyelids raised—God bless you both

My love to all
Your aff. son
O W H, Jr.

June 13, 1862[1]

My dear Father

Today's mail has made up for past injustice and neglect by bringing me five envelopes—4 enclosing letters and one, even better, a toothbrush—3 were from blushing maidens—I am glad you have rec'd mine if it were only to do our Regᵗ the justice of saying we were in some of the prettiest fighting—The 19th & Tammany[2] of our brigade weren't there but we were—And I wish that while *local* Regts like the 10th & 15th get cracked

[1] After the Battle of Fair Oaks, from June 1 to June 11, the Regiment remained in its advance position south of the Chickahominy. On the 11th it was relieved from the front line and moved a mile or so to high ground along the York River Railroad line, and established a camp there (Camp Lincoln).

[2] 42nd Regiment New York Volunteers.

up like thunder that the 20th got its due credit. At Ball's Bluff I think we fought better than the 15th Certainly our proportionate loss was greater *than any Regts in this whole army during the whole war*—at least I understand so—Our loss was more than one in 4 killed & wounded. And this time while we hear about the 10th &c &c & how the Tammany stood like veterans (two miles out of the fight) our work is hardly mentioned. After all it makes very little difference except for the sake of justice and one's friends. I wish you wouldn't all be so anxious—Our loss in this last fight of 25 K^d & W^d out of 400 (our whole fighting force) is about the usual proportion for the Regts actively engaged—

We are now for two days a little in the rear (about ¾ mile from the advanced pickets) our brigade having been relieved from the very hard work it or at least *we* have been doing.

For a week and a half mostly rainy—We had hardly any sleep hardly any blankets or anything—Shall I confess a frightful fact? Many of the officers including your beloved son have discovered themselves to have been attacked by body lice in consequence—(Caught perhaps from the men, perhaps from the dirty places we have been forced to live in or enter.) I shall fix their flints though now.

The men behaved like bricks through it all—I think my men like me—I have heard so—and I find the duties please me better than those of a Lt. My men cheered me after the fight. I have a 2nd Lt. with me by name

Murphy[3] who was a 1st Sergt—He was also 1st Sergt. of the small band who held Pickens under Slemmer[4] until Lincoln came into power & relieved them. He's a good soldier and a good fellow.

Well it's too hot to write more—

I have sent one or two notes since the one you rec'd to make sure you heard—& one for the Miff.[5] to Mother with permission to read—on the sly—It's queer that I stand this exposure and hard work better than many a stout fellow who looks more enduring than I.

I am always well and—as things are—contented—

Your loving son

O. W. Holmes, Jr. Capt. Co. G. XX Reg. Mass Hs.

I wrote you a letter in my pocket book while Sunday's fight was going on but didn't send it—as I wrote another more at length wh. you rec'd.

My love to all—

Tell Amelia & my friends to write—There is no other pleasure except receiving letters.

Don't want anything else

Send me some stamps also—& a paper of quinine.

[3] James Murphy.
[4] First Lieutenant Adam J. Slemmer.
[5] Not identified.

June 19. 1862[1]

My Dear Mother

I enclose a letter to Morse[2] which though not particularly interesting you may read. I will only add that in my own case the scorbutic symptoms are not as in general specific so much as they are disorders traceable to the same cause (want of *fresh* food) and wh. will I suppose be knocked in the head before they get much farther

It's rather funny to drink lemonade for disorder of bowels though! As the doctors order. The homesickness wh. I mentioned in my last they say is one of the first symptoms of scurvy. I have had very little more fresh food than my men so it would be natural to have the same troubles—

However I shall come out all right I don't doubt in a day or two.

Your Aff. Son
O W Holmes, Jr.

Send me the *Atlantic Monthly*

[1] The 20th Regiment was still encamped at Camp Lincoln on the York River Railroad.

[2] Presumably John T. Morse, Jr., Holmes's cousin and boyhood friend, and, later, biographer of Dr. Holmes.

[July 4, 1862
Harrison's Landing]¹

Dear Mother

We have had hard work for several days²—
marched all night—lain on our arms every morn'g &
fought every afternoon—eaten nothing—suffered the
most intense anxiety and everything else possible—I'm
safe though so far—But you can't conceive the wear &
tear—Lowell is probably dead bowels cut—³

Patten wounded leg⁴

Abbot   "   arm⁵

¹ The date of this letter is uncertain. It is likely, however, that it is
the letter referred to in the note dated July 4 as having been sent on
that morning. On July 4 the Regiment, with the rest of the Army of the
Potomac, was at Harrison's Landing on the James River.

² An account of the Seven Days Battle will be found in the letter
dated July 5, *infra* p. 58. Between June 19 and June 28 the Regiment had
remained on the alert at Camp Lincoln. On the 28th it was moved forward for the preparation of trenches. By that time the whole Army of
the Potomac, as a result of the engagements at Oak Grove (June 25), at
Beaver Dam Creek (June 26), and at Gaines's Mill, was on the South
side of the Chickahominy, and the line of communications with the
Pamunkey and York Rivers had been abandoned.

³ First Lieutenant James J. Lowell, commanding Company E, was hit
in the battle at Nelson's Farm on June 30 and died in the hands of the
Confederates. In his Memorial Day Address of May 30, 1884, Holmes
said of Lowell: "I see another youthful lieutenant as I saw him in the
Seven Days, when I looked down the line at Glendale. The officers were
at the head of their companies. The advance was beginning. We
caught each other's eye and saluted. When next I looked, he was gone."
—Holmes, *op. cit.* p. 6.

⁴ Second Lieutenant Henry L. Patten, Company E. Later, as Major of
the Regiment, he died of wounds received on September 13, 1864, at
Bailey's Creek.

⁵ First Lieutenant Henry L. Abbott had been wounded in the Battle
of Glendale.

Miller   "   & probably prisoner[6]
Our Co. had 9 or 10 wounded & some missing out of 37.

Give my love to all my friends & remember me in y'r thoughts & prayers—

Your loving Son
O W Holmes, Jr.

July 4. 62

Dear Mother

I sent a letter by a special messenger this morning & now enclose one by a wounded man whom if you see treat well—I only want to say I'm well after immense anxiety hardships & hard fighting—10 out of 37 wounded & some missing in Co G. I send a note I wrote in my pocket book some time ago (June 13—) to show my feelings—[1]

God bless you all infinitely

With my deepest love
Your Son
O W Holmes, Jr.

[6] First Lieutenant August Müller, Company E, was wounded and taken prisoner.

[1] On the back of the envelope enclosing this letter of July 4 appears a penciled notation in Holmes's hand, apparently written at a later date, stating: "letter referred to within destroyed—rather pompous."

July 5. 1862
[Harrison's Landing]

My Dear Mother and Father

June 29 we started from the trenches on our retreat—at Fair Oaks passed Rocket Guns & great quan-
tities of stores wh. had to be destroyed—Went a little
further & formed in line. Co^s I & B (the R. & Left. Co^s)
went out as skirmishers & my Co. as support Our own
side fired shell & cannister into us (hurt no one luckily)
and the 5th N. H. Regt. behaving badly I had to fall
back on the Regt. Afternoon marched to Savage's Stat^n
where lots more stores were destroyed and a hospital
stood where all the wounded had to be left to the enemy.
Here the enemy shelled us—Several men hurt none of
our Co. Major was touched but not hurt.[1] later there
was tall musketry (we sharing but little) and a South
Car^a Brigade[2] was chewed up.[3]

Marched all night* rested at early dawn—marched
and rested in woods noon—afternoon terribly thirsty
(hardly any water to be had) came up double quick

* rainy, but cleared up

[1] Major Paul Joseph Revere, as Colonel of the Regiment, was later
killed at Gettysburg. In Major Revere's own account of the engagement on the 29th he states that he was entirely uninjured, though he
lost two horses. See *A Memorial of Paul Joseph Revere and Edward
H. R. Revere* (Clinton, Mass., 1913), p. 131.

[2] Major General Joseph B. Kershaw's South Carolina Brigade.

[3] The battle on the morning of June 29 was fought at Allen's Farm;
the afternoon engagement was at Savage's Station. These two battles
and the engagement at Nelson's Farm on the 30th are together commonly known as the Battle of Glendale.

onto field of action (knapsacks on backs) Nelson's
Farm. Forward in line (whole battalion front) better
than the Regt. generally does it on drill—*Whang* goes
a shell two men drop in Co G. "Captain! Noonan's[4]
hit" "No Matter, Forward Guide Right" We go forward passing a deserted battery the dead lying thick
round it and then begins the deuce of a time the Mich.
7th on our left breaks & runs *disgracefully* (private) they
lay it to Col. Grosvenor[5] who they say showed the white
feather—Not a waver in our Regt. (Our Co. behaved
admirably better than most I may say) till Palfrey (Lee
comm'ded the Brigade & Dana the Divn pro tem.) gave
the order to march double quick in retreat We were
flanked & nearly surrounded and that saved us—After
that we couldn't avoid confusion and what with stragglers of other Regts &c. didn't form a good line—In our
Co. the loss in those known to be wounded was 1/5 to
1/4 the Co. not counting the missing of whose fate we
are ignorant nor those temporarily disabled only—as
one man stunned by a piece of shell for instance &
knocked out of fighting. The guns got so hot & dirty
we couldn't load or fire more than 2/3 of 'em. That
night June 30 we marched again (all this time I only
eating about 3 pieces of hard bread a [a] day & not want-
ing more hardly sleeping at all & never washing) We

---

[4] Private John Noonan, Company G, is not listed by Bruce in his history of the 20th Regiment as among the men wounded at Nelson's Farm.
[5] Colonel Ira R. Grosvenor commanded the 7th Regiment Michigan
Volunteers. He resigned his commission July 8, 1862.

started about I suppose as father was writing to me—
The next morn'g a splendid line of battle (of the whole
army) at Malverton where the Reb[s] shelled us (our
brigade) hard. The shell & Round Shot bounced round
lively. At midnight started and marched through terrible rain & mud till we reached the James. the next
afternoon. The anxiety has been more terrible than almost any past experience but through all I kept pretty
lively only getting down when on the last of our march
I was told by Cheerful birds like Tremlett & co that we
must surrender or be cut to pieces within 36 hours.

Poor Lowell was hit just as Willy Putnam was &
had to be left behind—beyond doubt dead. Patten hit
in leg. Abbot flesh w'd in arm. Muller wounded &
missing Palfrey bruised not hurt N. P. Hallowell cut
on the side not hurt. I was awfully frightened about
him—I'm in comm'd of E. & G. I'm too tired that is
too mentally inefficient to write well but I've sent 2
notes before including a leaf of my pocket book written
some time ago to you in case I was ever killed—If you
see Corpl. Johnson[6] Co G or any others of the Co.
treat 'em well—I gave Johnson a letter for you—*Never
give money—I protest against it most urgently*
          My love to all. All write please—

It was the thought of you dear ones sustained me in
terrible trials—Hereafter Allen's Farm, Savage's Sta-

[6] Corporal William A. Johnston of Company G had been wounded.
He was killed in action on May 18, 1864.

tion, Nelson's Farm, Malverton are added to my list of actions The hardest seems over now—at any rate I'm ready—

God bless you all
Goodbye
O W H, Jr.

Show this if you wish to any of my particulars Ellen Hooper[7] or any one—understanding it's *private* & not to be quoted—Keep all letters that are at all historical as I've no diary to speak of—
I hope that box hadn't gone Don't send it yet—

Sept. 5th 1862[1]
Washington.

My Dear Mother

I'm at the National Hotel being in town on 12 h'rs leave to get the necessaries of life which I've been without till now—I'm pretty well—*very* except for occa-

[7] Ellen Sturgis Hooper, sister of the future Mrs. Henry Adams, in 1868 married Professor Ephraim Whitman Gurney.

[1] During July the 20th Regiment, with the rest of the Army of the Potomac, remained at Harrison's Landing. On August 4 the Regiment had participated in the advance to Malvern Hill. Orders from Washington, however, compelled General McClellan to withdraw all his forces from the Peninsula and move them to join General Pope near Washington, which was threatened by General Jackson. Between August 16 and August 22 the Regiment marched from the James River to Newport News, via Yorktown. On the 25th the Regiment embarked at Newport News and arrived at Aquia Creek, on the Potomac, on August 27. After a number of long marches, the 20th Regiment finally encamped with the rest of the Second Corps at Tennallytown, Maryland, on September 4.

sional spasmodic pain in bowels & constant diarrhea wh. everybody has—I only write a word as I've a chance to stick it in the mail, to tell you that all the Regt. are O.K. & have had no fighting—Only been in reserve at one fight[2]—pickets &c. We're at Ten Alley Town (near George T.) ready to march in any direction we're wanted—Tell my friends I'll write at earliest opportunity.

Won't I have a good dinner today? perhaps not! I've spent $40. this morn'g already in refitting &c—

Yours most Afftly

Love to all   O W Holmes, Jr.

I came into Wⁿ with a private's blouse & trowsers—& now—my eye—the store clothes!

Sept. 17. '62[1]
Candle light

We have not been in any recent *fight*— 3 A.M. Beyond

Boonsburg—
Bivouac

Dearest Parents

I'm comparatively well though last night rain set me off again as usual Never since the terrible exposures

---

[2] In the neighborhood of Chantilly on September 1 and 2.

[1] Between September 5 and 17 the Regiment, with the rest of the Second Corps, had advanced from Tennallytown to a point beyond Boonsborough and Keedysville, near Antietam Creek. In this advance it had passed through Rockville, Hyattstown, Urbana, and Frederick City. The battle of Antietam occurred on the 17th.

of Fair-Oaks have I been myself—I can digest hardtack
or tacks or shingle nails but one damp night recalling
those dreary times plays the deuce with me—

Harris (H. & Chapman)[2] gave me a good mess for
the bowels in W[n] t'other day (when I spent 2 days &
about $80 & eat myself into a plethora*)—Well—
Hooker licked the Reb[s] nicely t'other day[3]—begun to
wax 'em I hear again last night—we're in reserve & near
to him & may fight today—expected to yesterday &
day before[4]—lick 'em if we do—D—n the N. Y. Herald[5]—Beastly news fr. Harper's ferry—Write just as
regularly (as you have *not* lately) whether I answer or

* Word not used medically—meaning unknown

[2] Theodore S. Harris was a member of the firm of Harris and Chapman, leading Boston apothecaries.

[3] Major General Joseph Hooker, commanding the First Corps, on September 14 had successfully participated in the engagement at Turner's
Gap in the course of the Battle of South Mountain. On September 16
General Hooker on the right wing of the Federal line had crossed Antietam Creek and engaged the enemy. The Twelfth Corps crossed on the
left the same evening.

[4] General Sumner, on Hooker's left, did not receive his orders to cross
the Antietam until 7 A.M. on the 17th, though, in accordance with orders,
he had his troops ready to advance across the creek at one hour before
dawn on the 17th.

[5] The *New York Herald* in mid-September, 1862, was vigorously criti-
cizing the radical, abolitionist, and "Jacobin" opposition to General
McClellan, was speaking most hopefully of the Maryland Campaign,
was making light of the Confederate successes around Harper's Ferry,
and in an editorial in the September 16th issue predicted that if
McClellan followed up his recent successes with a quick dash on Richmond, the rebellion might be brought to an end in sixty days. In the
September 17th issue the *Herald* played down the significance of the
Union surrender at Harper's Ferry on September 15 and took comfort in
its rumored evacuation by the Confederate forces just after the Federal
capitulation.

not—I want letters Just rec'd Ned's & Dad's Sept. 13—
All of us feel a deuced sight more like a fight than in that
forlorn peninsula. I don't talk seriously for you know
all my last words if I come to grief—You know my devoted love for you—those I care for know it—Why
should I say any more—It's rank folly pulling a long
mug every time one may fight or may be killed—Very
probably we shall in a few days and if we do why I shall
go into it not trying to shirk the responsibility of my
past life by a sort of death bed abjuration—I have lived
on the track on which I expect to continue travelling
if I get through—hoping always that though it may
wind it will bring me up the hill once more with the
deepest love

love to A. & N—

Your Son   W.

Sept. 18—[1862]

My Dear Parents

Once more I back it as per hint of yesterday's letter
—Usual luck—ball entered at the rear passing straight
through the central seam of coat & waistcoat collar coming out towa the front on the left hand side—yet it don't
seem to have smashed my spine or I suppose I should be
dead or paralysed or something—It's more than 24 h'rs
& I have remained pretty cocky, only of course fever-
ish at times—& some sharp burning pain in left shoulder

Pen & I singular to say are the hardest hit officers he
I think will lose his left arm—bone smashed above
elbow—We lay together for a while in a little house on
the field and were one time within the enemies lines,
heard their orders &c (they were all round us) but they
fell back & we escaped.[1]

[1] In Norwood P. Hallowell's *Reminiscences* (Privately Printed, 1897),
p. 16–18, he gives the following account of events after his wounding at
Antietam:
"Before long I gained the little farmhouse marked on the maps as the
Nicodemus house. The yard was full of wounded men, and the floor of
the parlor, where I lay down, was well covered with them. Among
others, Captain O. W. Holmes, Jr., walked in, the back of his neck
clipped by a bullet. The baggage train had not been up for many a
day, so that I had replenished my wardrobe by appropriation of chance
clothing from various sources. It so happened that I wore on that day
the light blue trousers and dark blue blouse of a private soldier. When
the rebels, a little later, were busy in the yard, paroling some and taking others to the rear, paying marked attention, of course to officers,
I was glad to have taken the precaution to remove my shoulderstraps
and to conceal them with my sword under a blanket.
"The first Confederate to make his appearance put his head through
the window and said: 'Yankee?' 'Yes.' 'Wounded?' 'Yes.' 'Would you
like some water?' A wounded man always wants some water. He off
with his canteen, threw it in the room, and then resumed his place in
the skirmish line and his work of shooting retreating Yankees. In about
fifteen minutes that good-hearted fellow came back to the window all
out of breath, saying, 'Hurry up there! Hand me my canteen! I am on
the double-quick myself now!' Some one twirled the canteen to him,
and away he went.
". . . For a while the farmhouse appeared to be midway between the
opposing forces. Shells broke the window panes, and ploughed up the
wounded in the yard, but not a shot went through the house.
"During some fifteen or twenty minutes only we were within the
rebel lines. Late that afternoon ambulances carried us off to Keedysville."
Events after the removal of Holmes from the Nicodemus house to
Keedysville are described in a letter from W. G. LeDuc to Holmes,
written in 1910. LeDuc, as Lieutenant Colonel and Quartermaster in

Only one doctor Haven the Surgeon of 15. Mass[2] has yet looked—he glanced hastily yesterday & said it wasn't fatal—I shall try to get home as soon as poss. but have no plans yet—

I shall write again soon—

Col. Revere is waiting for this[3]

Your loving

O W H, Jr.

General Dana's Brigade, was at Antietam and it was he who first notified Dr. Holmes of his son's wound. (See *My Hunt After "The Captain," op. cit. supra,* pp. 1-2.) In 1910, recalling the events at Antietam, LeDuc, speaking of Holmes in the third person, wrote as follows: ". . . when I was doing my level best to dress the wound and fix him up safe for the night or until a surgeon could take him in hand. 'I'm devilish glad it aint a case for amputation LeDuc for I haven't much confidence in your skill as surgeon.' . . . [We were at the house] where I exercised my clumsy surgery and where the mistress of the mansion when I ordered her to bring down her bigest [*sic*] & best feather bed and place it on the floor for this wounded officer objected in Pennsylvania idiom 'Nah I dinks not I prings mine fetter bet on dem floor,' I puts im on der petshtet'—'No that wont do I want it here where is plenty of fresh air.' 'Nah!'—'Well then I'll have to turn you all out and take your place for a hospital.' So the feather bed came, and the boy was washed as to wound and face and given an opium pill prescribed by old Doherty I think—and left in care of the dutchwoman and her children, no man was seen"—

It seems probable that the woman referred to by LeDuc was Margaret Kitzmuller, described by Dr. Holmes. (*Id.* p. 32.)

[2] S. Foster Haven, Jr.

[3] On September 4, 1862, Paul J. Revere, as Lieutenant Colonel, had taken up new duties as Assistant Inspector General of the Sixth Corps. He had been wounded at Antietam, where his brother, Edward H. R. Revere, Assistant Surgeon of the 20th, was killed. In April, 1863, he returned as Colonel to the 20th Regiment, following the resignation of Colonel Lee.

Hagerstown   Sept 22. [1862]

Per comissimam formosissimamque amanuensem
haec parentibus meis[1]

Tho unheard from I am not yet dead but on the
contrary doing all that an unprincipled son could do to
shock the prejudices of parents & of doctors—smoking
pipes partaking of the flesh pots of Egypt swelling round
as if nothing had happened to me.

I pulled up in good quarters at Hagerstown with
most charitable people of whom more anon & not feeling quite inclined to undertake the journey homeward
immediately alone—I decided to remain here a few days
from which determination my having a good time here
did not much detract In a day or two however I shall
start & I may remark I neither wish to meet any affectionate parent half way[2] nor any shiny demonstrations
when I reach the desired haven—

[1] The body of this letter is not in Holmes's handwriting. Anna Howell
Kennedy Findlay, the daughter of Holmes's hostess in Hagerstown,
Maryland, has described the young officer's visit in her article "Where
the Captain was Found," *Maryland Historical Magazine*, XXXIII (June,
1938), 109, 118, and has, perhaps, told of the occasion on which this
letter of September 22 was written:

"He dictated in Latin, a letter to his father; but she understood Latin
as well as he did, as she confessed when she cautioned him that he was
becoming a little too personal concerning herself in moods and tenses."

Mrs. Findlay identifies Holmes's amanuensis as Miss Ellen Jones of
Philadelphia.

[2] How ineffective this request was is known to all readers of Dr.
Holmes's *My Hunt After "The Captain,"* *loc. cit. supra*, originally published in the *Atlantic Monthly* in December, 1862. Dr. Holmes, as a
matter of fact, had left Boston on his hunt for the Captain on September 18.

Out of charity for you I will state plainly that I am really disgracefully well that I walk about all day & am in no respect in the condition of one who has been hit again within an inch of his life. I will be with you shortly for another jollification in Boston

Your loving Son

O. W. Holmes, Jr.

I only use an amanuensis from sheer laziness as I can write perfectly well my left arm only being a little paralyzed from the effects of my wound—

My right nerf hasn't forgot his cunning—[3]
Good news hyah!

[3] This phrase, the signature, and the two sketches were done by Holmes's hand.

Nov. 16(?) Sunday ev'g /62[1]
Warrenton—

My Dear Parents

We've got to Warrenton[2] & find the Corps is the Lord knows where—we shall have to retrace our steps to Catlet's St[a] leave our valises (perhaps to lose 'em) and start somewhither in the direction of Fredericksburg (?) Have been more or less blue of course but Abbott has made the journey easier & pleasanter.[3] Don't get in a pheeze We shall certainly hit the Reg[t] tomorrow and at any rate can take care of we—Hunting up a Regt isn't what it's cracked up to be and everyone seems to hold that you are a nuisance for [a] not having stayed at home as indeed but for honor I should suspect I was a fool—I believe it was best on the whole—but I have in fancy today been swelling on Beacon St. when I was in fact in beastly gov[t] cars smoking a T.D. & plug tobacco. We started at 11 AM & got here at 4½ PM Everything seems at 6[s] & 7[s] here & you see about as many secesh (I suppose paroled) swelling round as you do U.S. soldiers

[1] A part of Holmes's convalescence after Antietam seems to have been spent in Pittsfield. (See Carolyn Kellogg Cushing, "The Gallant Captain and the Little Girl," *loc. cit. supra*.) On an evening in early November or late October, however, he attended a dinner at the Parker House in Boston, at which ten officers of the Regiment, wounded or on leave, were present. See Bruce, *op. cit.* p. 180.

[2] Warrenton at this time was the Headquarters of the Army of the Potomac. On November 10 General McClellan had turned over command of the Army to General Burnside.

[3] Lieutenant Abbott had been at home on sick leave.

Keep your spirits up for "I love you still the same"
A. & I shall sleep out side the bed tonight for fear of
bugs—My eyes isn't everything shiftless nasty ill-condi-
tioned, mean & beastly—Wash^n stinks of meanness—it's
absolutely loathesome—Abbott & I are both of good
cheer—

Afftly Your Son
W.

Love to A. & E.[4]

Nov. 16 ? 1862
Sunday Ev'g—

This was begun to Emily Hallowell [1]
but I thought I'd write you instead—

My Dear Amelia

"Pity the sorrows of a poor" young "man"—After
being compelled to wait in Wash^n longer than we
wanted to—(for the utter absence of comfort is the least
fault of that modern Gomorrah) and after a night in
Alex^a, we started this morning at 11 A.M. & at 4½ PM
arrived at Warrenton, where we now are, only to find
that tomorrow we must go back to Catlet or Catnip or
something Station leave our valises perhaps forever &
wander off the Lord only (& no provost marshal)
knows where, in search of our vagrant Div^n There you

---

[4] On the back of the envelope appears the following: "Monday—
Chance of finding regt, rapidly diminishing."

---

[1] Sister of Captain Norwood P. Hallowell.

have our history thus far and now for the moral. While I'm living *en aristocrat* I'm an out-and outer of a democrat in theory, but for contact, except at the polls, I loathe the thick-fingered clowns we call the people—especially as the beasts are represented at political centres—vulgar, selfish & base—2ndly there are only two civilized places in America—Boston, known for its Statehouse and some cultivation, and Philad[a] celebrated for the Hallowells, cold slaw & large grained hominy—

Nov. 17. Monday ev'g—Today has been a day of trials —woke up at 6½ and found no landlord—last night he "doubted whether he sh'd be up to call us at 6 & they had only one nigger & in these days there was no making a nigger do anything"—We accordingly cleared out without paying a cent (wh., considering, we didn't much regret) got on to the last train fr. Warrenton (wh. we are leaving)—cars didn't stop at Catlet's—went 5 miles beyond—left valises (to be stored at Alex[a]) in charge of Rev[d] Fuller, brother of Marg[t], 16th Mass. V.[2] & walked back; at 2 P.M. tasted first food and water of today at camp of 16th Warrenton Junct[n]. & started cross country for main road to Fr'sburg—Went on spite of warning of some soldiers (pickets) about "gurillas" likely to pick us up—At dark (rainy) struck a nigger hut, but no road, & here we are, intending to pass

[2] Arthur B. Fuller, Chaplain of the 16th Regiment Massachusetts Volunteers, after resigning from the service on December 10, 1862, volunteered his services at Fredericksburg and was killed on the 11th.

night & I'm writing by light of the woodfire & the odd-
est resemblance of an antique Roman lamp I ever saw
it shows the origin [Sketch of lamp omitted.] It's going
out & I must stop—

Nov. 19. Yesterday was another direful day—A. & I
walked over 20 miles stopping occasionally at Secesh
houses & finally put up (after fears of camping out in
rain) at a good house with a motherly old gal who ad-
vised us to go home & get stronger. The women are
freeer in their expressions than the men & swear the
South will stick it out to the end—one of 'em had a
brother shot in the face before Richmond—This morn'g
went on on the dreary march, roads already getting
muddy & cut up—passed soldiers who of course quietly
sneered at us as straggling officers (a rare & disgraceful
sight) & had got on about 5 miles when we were ac-
costed by an old fella and lo! on t'other side of road
THE REGIMENT.[3] So here we are, a week after
starting & I'm writing by candlelight in Mason's[4] tent—
we move tomorrow but there's a rumor (very likely
false,) that we shall guard either Aquia or Fred'sburg—
Well I can't say but a word more now but imprimis
with the crack brained Dreher & obstinate ignoramus
Shepherd as act'g Col & Lt. Col.[5] the Regt is going

[3] On November 15 the 20th Regiment, with the rest of General Sumner's newly organized Grand Right Division, had left Warrenton and
had arrived at Falmouth, Virginia, on the 17th.

[4] First Lieutenant Herbert C. Mason.

[5] In the absence of Colonel Lee, who was in Boston on sick leave, and

to H——L as fast as ever it can or at least no thanks
to them if it isn't—I wouldn't trust it under them for a
brass tuppence in a fight—They'd send it to the devil
quicker even than Gen. Sumner and I've pretty much
made up my mind that the South have achieved their independence & I am almost ready to hope spring will see
an end—I prefer intervention to save our credit but believe me, we never shall lick 'em—The Army is tired
with its hard, & its terrible experience & still more with
its mismanagement & I think before long the majority
will say that we are vainly working to effect what never
happens—the subjugation (for that is it) of a great civilized nation. We shan't do it—at least the Army can't—
Well best dearest love to all

Your Aff. brother
W.

I'm well.

Nov. 20—Still rainy. had a bath & feel bully—only
moved a mile & have a good place here—

Friday
Still rainy Same place—Cold but well [6]

---

who never rejoined the Regiment, Captain Ferdinand Dreher as senior
Captain was temporarily in command of the Regiment. Captain Allen
Shepard, second ranking Captain, was acting Lieutenant Colonel of the
Regiment, Lieutenant Colonel Palfrey having been wounded at Antie-
tam. Palfrey never returned to active duty.

[6] On the back of the envelope enclosing this letter appears the following:

"Saturday—O.K. By and by send me a buffalo skin—it's very cold—
also silk h'dk'f *by mail* at once. I'll write for things as I want them."

Dec. 12. 1862.
Near Falmouth V^a
Hosp^1 20th Mass. V.

My Dear Mother
    (Show this to F. McG)

These have been very trying times for me I assure
you—First after being stretched out miserably sick with
the dysentery, growing weaker each day from illness
and starvation, I was disappointed in getting my papers
sending me to Philad^a by the delay at the various Head-
Q'rs & the subsequent business causing them to be over-
looked just as they reached the last—Sumner's—Then
—yesterday morng the grand advance begins[1]—I see
for the first time the Reg^t going to battle while I remain
behind[2]—a feeling worse than the anxiety of danger,
I assure you—Weak as I was I couldn't restrain my tears
—I went into the Hosp^1—the only tent left here—list-
less and miserable. They were just moving out a dead
man—while another close to death with the prevailing
trouble (dysentery &c.) was moaning close by—In the
Hosp^1 all day with no prospect of being moved or cared
for, and this morning we hear the Regt. has been in it.—
Exaggerated rumors; then it settles down that poor

[1] On Fredericksburg.
[2] At Fredericksburg the Regiment was under command of Captain
George N. Macy, with Captain Abbott acting as Major. It was on the
11th that the 20th made its memorable advance through the streets of
Fredericksburg. See footnote 5, *supra* pp. 40-41.

Cabot[3] is killed—and several, among them my 2nd Lt.[4] wounded—The cannonading of yesterday hasn't recommenced this morning but the day is young and I expect before night one of the great battles of the war[5]—I was on the point of trying to get down there but found I was too weak for the work—Meanwhile another day of anxious waiting—of helpless hopelessness for myself, of weary unsatisfied questioning for the Regt. When I know more I will continue my letter—I have no books I can read I am going to try to calm myself by drawing, but now four days have passed in disappointed expectations.—*Later*—

Dec. 13—Quiet all yesterday—Wrote James[6] in the afternoon (may not send it)—This morning there's heavy cannonading and just now there's a very lively musketry practise going on—and many a nice fellow going off, I doubt not. Still the popping keeps up lively but somehow it doesn't seem to settle down to a good steady roll—but it's brisk—Today will settle I fancy whether we fight more or not; if not whether it shall be one or two[7]—

[3] Captain Charles F. Cabot, Company F.

[4] Thomas M. McKay. McKay, when Captain of the company in the absence of Holmes, was assassinated on October 6, 1863.

[5] The operations on the 12th were directed principally to the movement of reinforcements across the Rappahannock.

[6] Not identified. It is unlikely that it refers either to William or Henry James, for there is no evidence of Holmes's friendship with either of them before 1864.

[7] On the 13th the costly effort to drive on beyond Fredericksburg towards Chancellorsville was unsuccessfully made. The 20th Regiment participated actively in this engagement.

Dec. 14. Today begun with a smart rattle but later the quiet has been oppressive—They fought all yesterday till after dark with great determination—Lt Willard[8] (late 1st Sergt Co D Capt. N. P. H.) & I climbed a neighboring hill & saw the smoke of the musketry; the flash of the shell as they burst; & the rest—We couldn't see the men but we saw the battle—a terrible sight when your Regt is in it but you are safe—Oh what self reproaches have I gone through for what I could not help and the doctor, no easy hand, declared necessary—And in it again the Regt. has been—Scarcely anyone now left unhurt Macy & Patten (Adj^t) Abbott & Murphy—these are all, as far as I can hear—The brigade went at an earthwork & got it with cannister—

Dec. 15. Last night a sharp volley probably from some Reg^t wh. got scared on picket—I rejoice to hear that in addition to the four mentioned as safe Mason & Ropes[9] are all right, also Perkins;[10] Half my company is wounded but none killed I judge from the serg't's report—

Lt. Alley[11]—Abbott's 2nd Lt. is killed—and I heard incidentally that the Revd Fuller (frère Margaret—who stowed our valises at W^n for us) had perished—Hayward they say looked like a butcher, red up to chin & elbows—

[8] Second Lieutenant Samuel Willard, later Captain, 54th Regiment Massachusetts Volunteers.

[9] First Lieutenant Henry Ropes, brother of Holmes's friend John Ropes, historian of the Civil War, was later killed at Gettysburg.

[10] Second Lieutenant William F. Perkins.

[11] Leander F. Alley was killed on December 13.

Mem. Pay F. W. Palfrey at once what I owe & apologise
for delay—twenty odd dollars—you'll find mem. in
one of the last pages of my old Mem. Book in Desk.
Send me a note of other debts on same page—I've *paid*
Lt. Milton[12] & the Sutler—*Owe* LeDuc,[13] Leech,[14]
F. W. P. Rec'd today LeDuc's letter & y'rs of Dec. 6.
but for some days at any rate mails will be shabby—
I shouldn't think we'd gained much as yet, unless Franklin has driven back their left a little[15]—I hear the Reb[s]
have warned our wounded out of Fred[s]burg & sure
enough the shelling on one side or both has just begun—
This is afternoon—you see I write a little from day to
day; it will be an interesting diary of one of the most
anxious and forlornest weeks of my military experience.
I'm not on the spot but I'll try to give an idea from
memory of the situation—

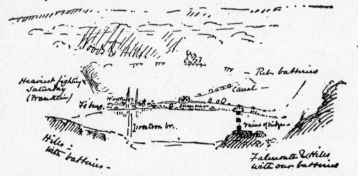

[12] First Lieutenant William F. Milton, of the 20th, had been wounded
at Antietam while serving as aide to General Dana.

[13] See footnote 1, *supra* pp. 65-66.

[14] Not identified.

[15] Major General W. B. Franklin was commanding the Left Grand
Division. All efforts to advance proved unsuccessful and on the night of

This isn't very correct[16] but will do to give an idea (gentle slopes from the Reb. batteries down to the River.) Well—yesterday the fellow I spoke of as near death the day of my going to Hospital, perished & there's another candidate now—Poor devils—there's little enough comfort in dying in camp except it be that one gets accustomed to it (as an Irishman might say) and has plenty of company—But it's odd how indifferent one gets to the sight of death—perhaps, because one gets aristocratic and don't value much a common life— Then they are apt to be so dirty it seems natural—"Dust to Dust"—I would do anything that lay in my power but it doesn't much affect my feelings—and so I'll stop for the present—

I include a letter to James & send this off hastily having a fair chance[17]—

The Regt. has been relieved I hear & is on this side—

Afftly

O W H, Jr.

December 16 the Army of the Potomac withdrew from Fredericksburg, and recrossed the Rappahannock to Falmouth.

[16] Other maps of Fredericksburg are at pp. 87-88 *infra*.

[17] On the back of the envelope was written: "I shall also want my new army shoes in my box."

Dec. 20. 62.
[Falmouth, Va.]

My Dear Governor

After the inspiration of a night which would have
been rather a nipper in your furnace-warmed house with
double glass, passed here with a couple of blankets in one
of the tents wh. I suppose Gen. Halleck (whom may the
Lord confound) would enumerate among the "luxuries"
of the Army of the Potomac—I sit down to give you the
benefit of my cheerfulness—I always read now the D.
Advertiser religiously as well as other papers—and I
was glad to see that cheerful sheet didn't regard the late
attempt in the light of a reverse—It *was* an infamous
butchery in a ridiculous attempt—in wh. I've no doubt
our loss doubled or tripled that of the Reb⁸. However
that's neither here nor there—I've just been reading
Mr. Motley's letters to Billy Seward[1] What a noble
manly high-toned writer he is—I always thought his
letters to you were more thoroughly what a *man* should
write than almost any I ever saw—I never I believe
have shown, as you seemed to hint, any wavering in my
belief in the right of our cause—it is my disbelief in our
success by arms in wh. I differ from you & him—I think
in that matter I have better chances of judging than
you—and I believe I represent the conviction of the
army—& not the least of the most intelligent part of it—

[1] On Monday, December 15, 1862, the *Boston Daily Advertiser* reprinted recent letters from John Lothrop Motley to Secretary Seward.
The letters dealt principally with affairs and attitudes in Austria.

The successes of wh. you spoke were to be anticipated as necessary if we entered into the struggle—But I see no farther progress—I don't think either of you realize the unity or the determination of the South. I think you are hopeful because (excuse me) you are ignorant. But if it is true that we represent civilization wh. is in its nature, as well as slavery, diffusive & aggressive, and if civ^n & progress are the better things why they will conquer in the long run, we may be sure, and will stand a better chance in their proper province—peace—than in war, the brother of slavery—brother—it is slavery's parent, child and sustainer at once—At any rate dear Father don't, because I say these things imply or think that I am the meaner for saying them—I am, to be sure, heartily tired and half worn out body and mind by this life, but I believe I am as ready as ever to do my duty— But it is maddening to see men put in over us & motions forced by popular clamor when the army is only willing to trust its life & reputation to one man—

Please send me by mail 6 of the best kind of $photog^s$ of me—(the 2/3 lengths—they are stunners—I think I'd rather play my game with that dummy than in person)—I want to give them to some of the officers—By Ged (the vowel is an *E*) the Reg^t did behave gloriously in the late *rumpi*. I feel a sort of dispassionate pride combined with my regret at my own absence—Isn't this a bully kind of a letter—I shall get Patten to direct it so that you may think it a bill [2]—

[2] The address on the envelope is not in Holmes's handwriting.

OLIVER WENDELL HOLMES, JR.

The groaning board calls me—in fact it howls—"To dinner" A bully dinner today—beefsteak (fried) beans (stewed—baked unknown) & rice—Hyah!

Dinner's over—the beefsteak was broiled on the coals not fried and for the 1st time for 2 weeks I've eaten my belly full and any animal food to speak of—10 to 1 it makes me sick—

My love to all—Oh—please send me also by mail—books go cheap—Cairnes' book—Amer. Ed[n] [3]

Your Aff. Son
O W Holmes, Jr.

[3] Presumably John Elliott Cairnes, *The Slave Power* (2nd ed.; New York, 1862), the London edition of which was reviewed in the *Atlantic Monthly* for September, 1862.

LETTERS, MARCH 1863—APRIL 1864

March 18, 1863[1]
[Falmouth, Va.]

5.[2] I can have a comfortable P.S. on decent paper—
Since I was last at Sedgwicks to see Whit.[3] (HdQrs 6th
Corps) Sedgwick said to Whit. "Tell Capt Holmes he
must come over again soon I want to hear him talk" or
words to that effect. Likewise if a certain party didn't
get a Comm'n as Major and go on his staff he asked
Whit. how would the Captain like the place to wh. W.
very properly responded that I wouldn't take it—But
fr. this things [*sic*] I fancy old John rather likes me &
you must know that John Sedgwick is one of the biggest
Maj. Gen[ls] now in our army—Today it was suggested
to me (as it has previously been also to Ropes (Lt.)) that
I sh'ld take Prov. Ml[s]Ship of Corps wh. also I politely

---

[1] Early in January, 1863, Holmes had apparently been on sick leave in
Philadelphia where he was visited by his parents. (See Ralph L. Rusk,
The Letters of Ralph Waldo Emerson (New York, 1939), V, 305.) On
January 25, 1863, the 20th Regiment moved into the town of Falmouth
and took over duty as provost guard. Holmes, who presumably had returned to duty by then, was appointed Provost Marshal of the town.
Colonel Lee had resigned his command, and though Lieutenant Colonel
Palfrey was promoted to fill the vacancy, he was unable to report for
duty. Captain Macy acted as regimental commander until the middle of
April when Colonel Paul J. Revere took the command. On January
28 General Burnside had been removed from the command of the Army
of the Potomac, and General Hooker succeeded him. General Sumner
also resigned at that time, being replaced by General Couch. The
Grand Divisions, established by Burnside, were dissolved and the organization of the Army into Corps reëstablished.

[2] The main body of the letter has apparently been destroyed.

[3] Captain Charles A. Whittier, previously in Holmes's company of the
20th, had been assigned as A.D.C. to General Sedgwick, commanding the
Sixth Corps.

declined—I should like a good staff appointment but I wouldn't leave the Regt. I tell you these things because you like to hear 'em & Sedgwicks talk did tickle me a little (though it only showed personal liking)—The latter merely came fr. Maj. Mallon[4] who is now Prov. M[1] 2nd Corps & Lt. Potter[5] (son of Bishop) who wanted some one & knew that the 20th were A.1. and that our crowd was a pleasant one—

Yr Loving Son
O W H, Jr.

Falmouth V^a/
Mar. 29—'63

My Dear Old Dad

I had my blowoff in one of my last and now let bygones be bygones—if *you* will—for I fear I was somewhat in the mood wh. would have led to sass had I been at home—Imprimis—I send two sketches of Fred[s]burg by Col. Hall who, thank the Lord, has returned to the Brigade—also a rough one of FairOaks wh. he surveyed & mapped out[1]—

[4] James E. Mallon of the 42nd Regiment New York Volunteers served as Provost Marshal of the Second Corps under General Couch. He was later killed while commanding his Regiment at Bristoe Station in October, 1863.

[5] First Lieutenant James Nelson Potter, son of Bishop Alonzo Potter.

[1] The maps are reproduced at pp. 87-89. Colonel Norman J. Hall had been in command of the 3rd Brigade, 2nd Division at Fredericksburg.

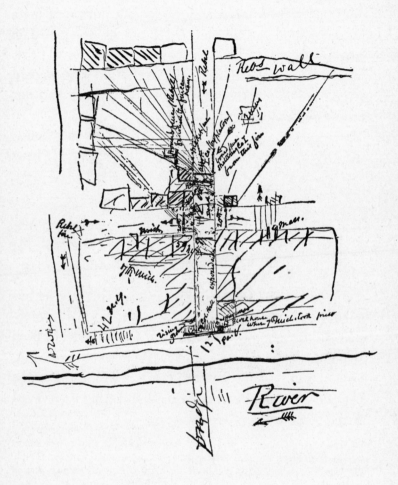

88

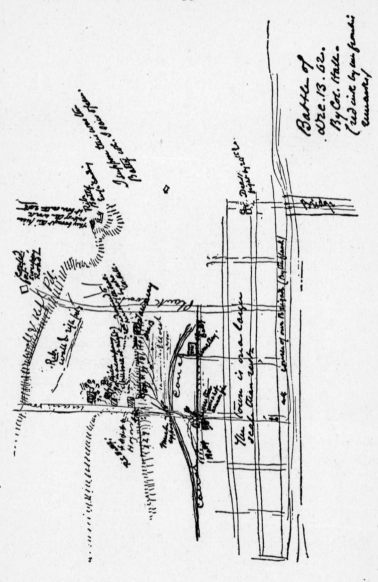

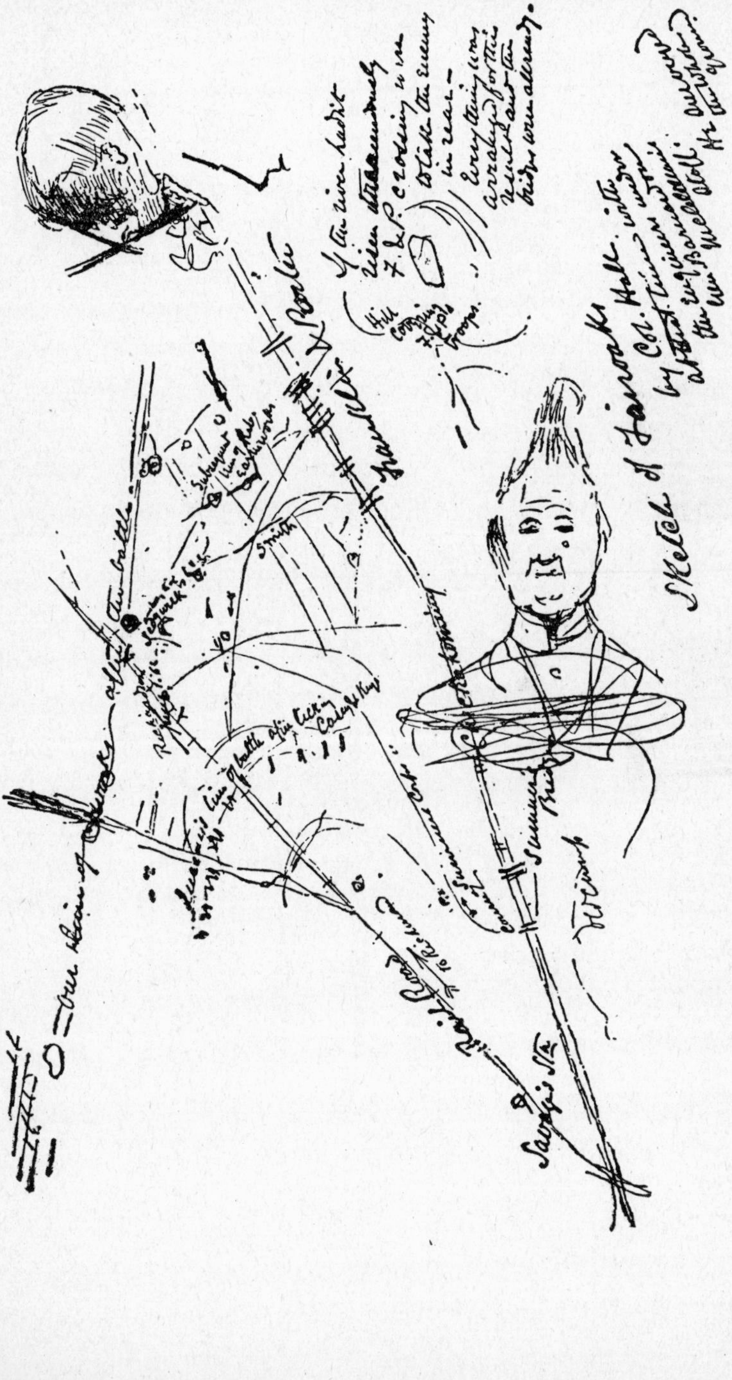

Sketch of Fairoaks
by Col. Hall
Rail Road
To Richmond
Savage's Sta
Franklin & Porter
Smith
Summer's Bridge
Chickahominy
after the battle
Hill
Troops
If the river had'nt risen tremendously F. & P. crossing was to take the enemy in rear — Everything was arranged for this result and the bridges were already.

What a joy it is to have a man thoroughly educated to his biz. wellbred, knowing what's what & imparting his knowledge in place of one who tells you his Reg^t * (not such a remarkable one except for a P^{enn} Regt) has been in 42 battles & other unending blowing about himself, it, and the transcendent merits of both—Not that Brooke[2] was as bad as some either. I was talking to Hall about this *blowing* being something I didn't much like or understand & he said "Yes your Regt is more like old times" (meaning thereby the old Regular Army where Officers *were* Gentlemen) "than anything I have seen in the Army." wh. in connection with other remarks about the perfection of their present condition and their behavior in the Field rather pleased me—He said "The 20th have no poetry in a fight" and there *is* about as little excitement & hullabulloo on those occasions as may be—At F^{s}burg (see 1st Map) Macy says quietly "Mr Abbot you will take your first platoon forward" to wh. A. "1st Platoon forward—March" and walks quietly ahead—His 1st Platoon is knocked to pieces (He lost that day 30 out of 60—10 shot dead) instantly—"You'll have to put in the 2nd" says Col. H. "2nd Platoon forward" and A. leads them too into the storm with the same semiindifferent air that he has when drilling a Batt^n. I really very much doubt whether there is any

* 53^d P^a V.

[2] Colonel John R. Brooke commanded the 53rd Regiment Pennsylvania Volunteers, which was actively engaged at Fredericksburg.

Reg^t wh. can compare with ours in the Army of the Potomac. Everyone says this, perhaps, who belongs to a good Reg^t but still I fancy I am right from the evidence of many things.

Now I fancy the time is counted by days almost, rather than by weeks, before we move—and by weeks only before we fight[3]—

Ah well, I am trying to see things straight in my own mind before it all begins so as to be ready and cheerful—

I am a little totty bit melancholy just now but that will soon be gone as it is only a passing cloud. It's very well to recommend theoretical porings over Bible & Homer—One's time is better spent with Regulations & the like and any connected study situated as I am is rather impossible. What I do read is chiefly connected with War and Fiction[4]—

[3] At this point the balance of the page was torn off.
[4] Here the same tearing off as that referred to in the preceding footnote has destroyed the balance of the letter.

May 3. [1863][1]

Dear Mother

Ned Paine arrived here last night & is at present oc-
cupied in his maiden battle—if not killed [2] Pour moi I'm
already hit in the heel—bullet fr. spherical case—

Pleasant to see a d'd gun brought up to an earthwork
deliberately brought to bear on you—to notice that your
Co. is exactly in range—1st discharge puff—second puff
(as the shell burst) and my knapsack supporter is
knocked to pieces (Mem. We are lying down) 2nd discharge man in front of me hit—3d whang the iron enters
through garter & shoe into my heel—

They have been firing hard ever since & as the
stretcher is waiting for me I stop—

Your loving
O W Holmes, Jr.

later I've been chloroformed & had bone extracted—
probably shant lose foot[3]

[1] During the latter days of April successful opening moves in the
Chancellorsville campaign were made by General Hooker. The 20th
Regiment, part of Gibbon's Division of the Second Corps remained at
Falmouth during these operations. On the night of May 2-3, however,
it moved forward, and the morning of the 3rd the Regiment crossed the
Rappahannock, passed through Fredericksburg, and approached the canal
to the west of the town. It was while waiting there to effect a crossing
of the canal that the Regiment came under Confederate artillery fire
from Marye's Heights as described in this letter.

[2] Second Lieutenant Sumner Paine, recently commissioned from civilian life and first cousin of Holmes, was killed at Gettysburg, July 3, 1863.

[3] The bottom of the page, which may possibly have contained further
writing, has been torn off.

May 4. 63
Lacy House

In case my letter of yesterday shouldn't arrive I send you my programme—

I purpose as soon as poss. to get on to Phil^a if I don't get leave to go soon though I shall send my med. certif— & request you to go to the Surg. Genl at W^n & get my leave—

The bullet hid itself in the os calcis

Feel pretty well but bored to death & fed on pap—

O W Holmes, Jr.

Capt. Murphy is hit[1]—all the rest are well so far— Hayward is at work here

May 4. 63

Dear Father

I've written two or three epistles wh. I suspect will not reach you & so write again—I'm hit in the heel—ball (from sperical [*sic*] case) buried in Os Calcis—chloroformed & ball extracted—foot didn't have to come off as was feared—

I shall start for Phil^a as soon as I can get my leave—

Love to all

O W Holmes, Jr.

Murphy flesh wound in arm
No one else hurt.

[1] James Murphy, Company F.

Feb. 1, 1864[1]

Dear Father

Please see the Paymaster in Boston Major Robie[2] or Amory[3] or whoever pays Volunteers in Boston now, *at once*—& ask him to what time I have been paid.—Tell him there is no note on my leave of absence of pay[t] beyond April 30th 1863.[4] But I think or had the impression I had been paid later—let me know the answer without delay & oblige y'r loving

O W H Jr.
A.D.C. Brig. Gen[l] H. W. Wright
Comd[g] Div[n] 6th Corps
Washington D. C.

Inclosed papers to be stowed in 2nd drawer in closet—

[1] The exact date and circumstances of Holmes's return to active duty following his convalescence from his Fredericksburg wound have not been ascertained. The records of the Adjutant General in Washington indicate that he was put on detached service from the 20th Regiment as A.D.C. to Major General Horatio G. Wright, commanding the 1st Division of the Sixth Corps by orders dated February 2, 1864. Presumably this letter of February 1 was written shortly before or after Holmes's arrival at Divisional Headquarters. John C. Ropes, writing from Boston to Major John C. Gray on January 9, 1864, said that Holmes had "gone back." (See *War Letters, 1862-1865, of John Chipman Gray and John Codman Ropes* (Boston, 1927), p. 274.) In the Diary of First Lieutenant Charles W. Folsom, quartermaster of the 20th, which is preserved in the Regimental collection at the Boston Public Library, there is an entry dated January 8, 1864, stating that Holmes is back. It is evident, accordingly, that for a part of January he was with his Regiment in the neighborhood of Stevensburg above the Rapidan River. Major Abbott at the time was in command of the Regiment.

[2] Major Frederick Robie.

[3] Perhaps Colonel Charles Amory, Master of Ordnance, of the Commonwealth.

[4] Traces of this dispute as to an alleged overpayment to Holmes appear among Holmes's papers down to 1886.

Apr. 18: 1864[1]

I have you scout the possibility of the human reason ever conceiving that $\begin{cases} 1+1=3 \\ 2+2=5 \end{cases}$—and further deny the possibility of the truth of that proposition—This of course involves the assumption of certain fixed principles in reason wh. cant be disturbed by any education —i.e. independent of the senses & if true proves their existence—So we may suppose a reasoning being to whom the only *external*—(objective) matters perceptible were like Boskevitch's (is that the Dutchman's tarnal name?) conception of the original atoms *viz.* (polar) centres of force of the nature of mathematical points—Let this force be gravitation—Two of these points being brought into such correlation in space as to admit of both being perceived at once are found like double stars to establish a third point—a *centre of gravity* & having the same relations to point 4 if it appears that p^t 1 has to pt 2.—around wh. each revolves— but unlike the case of double stars the two original points are immaterial and like the 3^d

Then the only case wh. our senses would present us of the juxtaposition of one perceptible to a second would be a case of 3 perceptibles—As it is now we can put one apple by another apple & no 3^d apple invariably ranges in row—but supposing our uniform experience were as I have imagined shouldn't we say $1+1=3$?

[1] This portion of the letter dated April 18, 1864, is all that has been preserved.

Answer me this riddle which with delight I concocted
to stick my daddy et eris mihi magnus Apollo—

[Undated—1864 (?)][1]

The being whom we have supposed does not per-
ceive a & b except in relation or as you express it as 1×1.
but 1×1 i.e. force p^t a in dynamical relation with force pt
b begets force p^t c and as the being supposed never per-
ceives a & b except with c he will have no idea of a & b
without c (for having only one sense he can't correct its
impressions from the data of any other as we can) or
[or] of $1+1=2$ but only of $1+1=3$ a+b+c
The answer is as follows—if the hypothesis of the single
sense means only the fact gravitation rendered into consciousness then $a \times b$ (i.e. *a* in dynam[1] relat[n] with b) will
affect the consciousness as they would a new force p^t—
consciousness of force points a & b will be obliterated &
taken up in a new consciousness viz. *single* force point *c*
wh. $= a+b$—
You don't answer the puzzle but fall into the trap &
confess $1+1+(1 \times 1)=3$ i.e. that 1 & 1 in the only relation *con*ceivable to our friend the unisensate because the
only *per*ceivable $=3$—In fact $1+1=1$ *twice as big* like
2 raindrops coalescing as I've shown on the hypothesis

[1] This note on a small scrap of paper, bears no date. It has been
placed here because it deals further with the subject discussed in the
note of April 18, 1864, and was presumably written at approximately the
same time.

wh. I put forward & you fell into like a stult—there w'd
be a true case of genesis of force if unfortunately the
hypothesis were not absurd—in imagining him to per-
ceive a & b & at the same time c—The absurdity of my
attempt was that I tried starting from an hypothesis consistent with the data (i.e. all our experiences of externals
& all *conceivable exper.* <u>*consistent with*</u> our past experiences) which even I granted uniformly taught
$1+1=2$ to deduce an inconsistent result—

DIARY AND LETTERS, MAY 3—JULY 1864

May 3ᵈ 1864[1]

Rec'd this,[2] April 29—nothing very particular to record as yet—Read Gen. Morris's book[3] for evolutions by a flank—("Column of fours"—) We need a good book of this sort. This book however is not very good— The orders are poor (I think) & sometimes absolutely incorrect or contrary to the spirit of Tactics.

Rec'd, yesterday, letter fr. F. B. D.[4]

Also my boy Lewis, having rec'd his last month's wages and agreed to stay with me, cut stick—This morn'g a note goes to Col. Ewing 4th N. J. V.[5] to arrest him if there as I suspect he is. Notified Prov. Ml.— We (Hayden[6] & I) are reciting Tactics in review. Yesterday the Gen. reviewed & inspected the 3d Brig. (Russell's)[7]—This is the last Review & Inspection of the series we have been having. There are some fine fighting Regts in this Brig. e.g. the 6th Maine—But none of them are first rate—hardly 2nd rate—in soldierly appearance & setting up—or, I suspect, in discipline—

[1] At this time the Sixth Corps was encamped near Walford's Ford on the Hazel River above Culpepper Court House.

[2] This presumably refers to the small notebook in which the diary was recorded.

[3] Presumably Brigadier General William Hopkins Morris, *Field Tactics for Infantry* (New York, 1864).

[4] Fanny Bowditch Dixwell.

[5] Lieutenant Colonel Charles Ewing.

[6] Presumably Captain T. L. Haydn, A.D.C. to General Wright.

[7] The 3rd Brigade of the 1st Division was commanded by Brigadier General David A. Russell.

Of Shaler's 3 Regts[8] all poor & damned scraggly, the best was the 65th N. Y.—The Jersey Brig.[9] all through showed good and serviceable stock—The [sic] was the handsomest appearing. Already they need Torbert[10]—Upton's Brigade[11] appeared well, in connection with his handsome camp. The 121st N. Y. afterwards went through the manual very nicely—some fancy dodges—

H.Q. 1st Div. 6th Corps
10 P.M. May 3, 1864

Dear Parents

In six hours we start[1]—at 4 A.M. tomorrow—You won't get this I suppose for some time—I sent my diary[2] a week or more ago & judge by Amelia's letter (Rec'd today—telling of serenade &c) it hasn't been rec'd—*Be sure to get that when* the mails are forwarded—This is only a parting word of love to all at home—

[8] Brigadier General Alexander Shaler's 4th Brigade was constituted of the 65th, 67th, and 122nd Regiments, New York Volunteers, and the 23rd and 82nd Regiments Pennsylvania Volunteers.

[9] The 1st Brigade (Jersey) at this time was commanded by Colonel Henry W. Brown.

[10] At this time Brigadier General A. T. A. Torbert was commanding the 1st Division in General Sheridan's Cavalry Corps. Torbert, as Colonel, had commanded the 1st Brigade in General Slocum's division of the Sixth Corps in the fall of 1862.

[11] Colonel Emory Upton commanded the 2nd Brigade of the 1st Division. The 5th Maine, 121st New York, 95th and 96th Pennsylvania Volunteer Regiments constituted Upton's Brigade.

[1] On the Wilderness Campaign.

[2] This Diary has not been found.

I suppose we fight in a day or two—Till then goodbye—I have no new words of affection now—I am well
and in excellent spirits—

Your loving

O. W. Holmes, Jr.

I shall see the fight on the Staff in every probability—
My love to Amelia, Ned, and doubly to each of you—

[DIARY]

May 4—At 4 a.m., nominally, we started on the Spring
Campaign—Got up at 3 & under weigh about 6.
Marched by Brandy St[a] & Stevensburg to Germanna
Ford—following 5th Corps[1]—Crossed by one wooden
& one canvass pontoon bridge—and I write this in camp
about a mile & a half from the Ford. Yesterday bought
Rice's[2] mare for $150.

Morn'g at first cold then cool & at noon quite hot—
Lee is said to be concentrating at Mine Run—Hancock[3] at Chancellorsville. Warren at Mine Run. It is
said we shall take up position about 5 miles from here—
Our Div[n] marched quite well. Some of the troops however straggled a good deal. Many of the stragglers had
preposterous loads on their backs & many of the lame
ducks wore boots.

[1] Major General G. K. Warren was commanding the Fifth Corps.
[2] Not identified.
[3] Major General W. S. Hancock was commanding the Second Corps.

Almost everyone including me had a headache by the
end of the march—

Saw Col. W. F. Bartlett [4] just long enough to say
glad to see you.

May 5th.

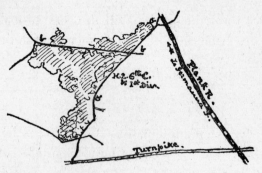

At daybreak advanced along Plank road with flankers
out on our right—then advanced in line along road *a a*—
southwesterly—Upton trying to connect with 5th
Corps on his left—Some trouble in keeping connection
between Upton (left—) Brown (N. J. Brig.) & Russell (right)—(Shaler with the wagon trains—) The
orders were to touch to the left & regulate the advance
by the right. Skirmished forward 1½ m.

At one point Gen. Sedgwick's & Gen. W's HdQrs.
were very accurately shelled from the left—one struck
within a yard of quite a number of us who were sitting
on horseback & bounced under the horses—Others

[4] Bartlett at this time commanded the 57th Regiment, Massachusetts
Volunteers, which was included in the 1st Brigade, 1st Division, of the
Ninth Corps.

threw fragments round constantly for a few minutes &
as a Regt. was filing by to the right a shell or roundshot
striking in it covered many of the staff with brains[5]—
Finally established H.Q. at point H. 2.—Evening attempted an attack unsuccessfully—The 2nd line
got flurried and begun firing into the first, and break-
ing—But Genl[s] [sic] W., Duffy,[6] & the rest of the staff
soon restored order—(This is written up May 11, I
leave a space for additions)—Macy was with us but
left as soon as Hancock connected—

1st Div.   6th Corps
May 6th 1864   5.15 o'clock, PM.

Dear Parents

Second day of battle Not done yet—I am all right &
Whit & Dalton[1]—I hear Macy wounded in shoulder[2]
Abbott wounded *severely* don't know where[3]—

[5] For another account of this incident, see Thomas W. Hyde, *Following the Greek Cross* (Boston, 1894), pp. 184-185.
[6] Probably Lieutenant Colonel James N. Duffy, Acting Inspector General, 1st Division of Sixth Corps.

[1] Presumably Major Henry R. Dalton, Assistant Adjutant General
of the 1st Division, Sixth Corps.
[2] Colonel George N. Macy was wounded on May 6 while commanding
the 20th Regiment which was in the 1st Brigade of the 2nd Division of
the Second Corps.
[3] Abbott assumed command of the Regiment when Colonel Macy was
wounded. Shortly afterwards Abbott was fatally wounded.

Col. Frank Bartlett wounded in head—20th said to be comm'ded by 1st L^t—

Your loving

O W H, Jr.

It is doubtful if you get this A Tribune Corr^t. will try to get it through—
Considerable firing & yells now—

[DIARY]

May 6—(Hot but fine day)

A simultaneous attack was tried at 5 a.m. advanced some way—not much effected however—a marsh, abattis & battery in our front—Gen. W. managed to keep himself & staff pretty well in range of their shells—Lost some prisoners stuck up to waist in marsh, in their attempt to charge—Seymour[1] tried to advance 7.40 a.m. but found himself outflanked—

Our H.Q. were exposed all day to pretty sharp art^y practice from 3 different directions partly drawn by the sight of our horses—several horses & men hit.

At dusk after a brief picket fire & just as Gen. Sedgwick was expressing apprehensions and sending* to reinforce the right the enemy flanked & broke Seymour & Shaler—& there was a stampede of these Brig-s. back to plank road—Seymour prisoner, Shaler missing—

* (Gen. S. had ordered over 2 Regts—)

[1] Brigadier General Truman Seymour commanded the 2nd Brigade in the 3rd Division of the Sixth Corps. General Shaler also was taken prisoner.

We all tried to rally the troops but in vain—Rice
wounded[2]—The enemy apparently came in by road *bb*
(p. 2.) [p. 104 *supra*.]
(Mem. May 16. I see the papers esp. Tribune[3] mention very complementarily conduct of Staff of Gen[s]
Sedgwick & Wright)
(See A & N Journ. I p. 646.[4] Gordon's Brig.[5] turned
our right)—

May 7.
Up all night in the saddle—establishing new line—
our right (Russell) resting on plank road—Gen. Neill [6]
on right of the road—Cavalry sent up the road, but got
stampeded & mizzled—About 4 am. Farrar[7] & I fell in
with McCartney's Batt[y8] on the road and he gave us a

[2] This perhaps refers to Brigadier General James C. Rice, commanding
the 2nd Brigade of the 4th Division, Sixth Corps, who though not
wounded actively participated in the engagement of the 6th. He was
killed on May 10.

[3] In the *New York Daily Tribune* of May 10, 1864, there appeared a
dispatch from its field correspondent, Charles A. Page, dated May 6,
11 P.M., giving an account of the opening phases of the Wilderness
Campaign. Its penultimate paragraph concluded:
"I may not refrain from mentioning for gallantry, Sedgwick's staff and
Wright's."

[4] In the *Army and Navy Journal* for May 21, 1864 (I, 646), there is reprinted an account of the Battle of the Wilderness from the *Charleston
Mercury* of May 10.

[5] Brigadier General John B. Gordon's Brigade at the time was in the
Division of Major General Robert E. Rodes.

[6] Brigadier General Thomas H. Neill commanded the 3rd Brigade in
General Getty's 2nd Division (Sixth Corps).

[7] Presumably Major Henry W. Farrar, who at this time was on the
staff of General Sedgwick, commanding the Sixth Corps.

[8] Captain William H. McCartney commanded the 1st Battery (Battery
A) of the Massachusetts Light Artillery.

wash & a breakfast—Found Gens. S. and W. just afterwards—No fighting, except picket firing, on line of
6th Corps. Horse got his only feed for 36 hours in the
am.—

Not much except picket firing today—

Orders to march at 8½ P.M. postponed to 9½ P.M.
Were on the road all night.

This day was very fatiguing—my heart beat strangely
& I felt somewhat as I remember doing at Harrison's
Landing[9]—

Lee started within an hour of the time we did, they
say, & we taking all night to make Chancellorsville L.
was enabled to get to Spottsylv^a C^t H^s just ahead of us,
marching by a parallel road—I suppose the "Brook
Road"—I think this was discreditable to us—

May 8th

At daylight made Chancellorsville passing 9th C. &
Burnside[10]—Road crowded with (Supply) Trains and a
long line of Ambulances which the enemy's holding
Ely's Ford prevented starting for Rapp^k St^a with Ned
Dalton[11] in charge—as it was intended they should the
evening before.

Stopped at Piney Br. Church for troops to breakfast—
Advanced turning to left at church. After going a mile

---

[9] The 20th Regiment had gone to Harrison's Landing in July, 1862,
after the Peninsula Campaign.

[10] General Burnside commanded the Ninth Corps.

[11] Major Edward B. Dalton was Surgeon with the Army of the Potomac.

or 2 found woods afire & bodies of Reb^s & our men just
killed & scorching—just as we were forming a line of
battle Warren sent word he was hard pressed & Gen. W.
sent forward all but Upton Brig. of his Div. Art^y remained behind—I was sent to notify Gen. Sedgwick—
looked in vain for him at H.Q.A.P. & got snubbed by
Gen. Meade[12]—After seeing Gen. S. returned to front
so tired I could hardly sit up—got a little coffee en route
fr. one of McCartny's Lieuts.

Orders for gen^l attack towards sunset—it begun on
our left (Warren) & we were to take up the movement
—some good charges but it didn't result in much—
sharpshooters, annoyed apex of angle of crotchet on
right of our Divⁿ.

It is said that Longstreet's Corps only was pres^t when
Warren was licked—

May 9*th*
Notes for this day lost—
Morn'g 1st Div. passed from Warren's right to his left
to rejoin Corps—We had just arrived when Whittier
rode up to Gen. W. with news that Sedgwick was
killed—we had been with him a moment before—he
was in an exposed angle between Warren's front & ours
& had just been chaffing a man for ducking at the bullets
of a sharpshooter; saying "Why man they couldn't hit
an elephant here at this distance"—he was struck on one

---

[12] Major General George G. Meade was in command of the Army of
the Potomac under Grant.

side of the nose & sunk senseless & soon died—
McMahon[13] & Whittier were with him at the time—

Gen. Wright took the Corps by comm^d Gen. Meade although Ricketts[14] ranked him—Nothing in particular except advancing pickets—reconnoisances &c I believe during today—(Written up 6 P.M. May 16.)

May 10.

Up about 4 a.m.—turned in at 12 for little sleep—pickets firing tumultuously every little while[15]—

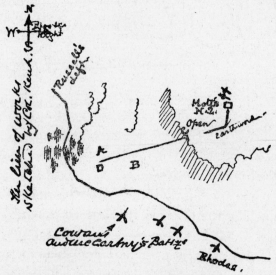

The points of compass are about right. No attempt to indicate distances.

[13] Lieutenant Colonel Martin T. McMahon, Assistant Adjutant General of the Sixth Corps.

[14] Brigadier General James B. Ricketts commanded the 3rd Division of the Sixth Corps.

[15] The Battle of Spottsylvania opened on May 10.

Gen. Mott[16] was expected to push along Russell's[17] front in a S. direction—

At *A* the road starts from the little house ☐ apparently nearly parallel with the earthworks—but bears away in a general direction of about E. by N. At *B* the troops were massed previous to the afternoon attack. At *C* woods-end—Mott's breastworks are in the open— they should be on a prolongation of A C about 2 or 3 times as far off as represented—

The gateposts at *C* are nearly N. & S.

About 11 a.m. went out to Gen. Mott in position above indicated to make him press the enemy more vigorously in a S. dir[n] toward our right—He seemed somewhat stupid and flurried. Told him to assure his connection with Russell by moving a little forward and prolonging toward his right—and then to feel with & press forward his left. He had attacked with three Regts by His Right—& one regt. was broken—they found an earthwork & grape across an open field—This work must be enfiladed by Cowan[18] & McCartny—

On returning found Grant, Meade, Humphreys[19] et al. big bugs & had the honor of a word with Grant & a shake of the hand from Meade—Roundshot, Shell, & a few shots from Sharpshooters flew round loose as I rode

[16] Brigadier General Gersham Mott commanded the 4th Division in Hancock's Second Corps.

[17] General Russell had succeeded General Wright as commanding general of the 1st Division.

[18] Captain Andrew Cowan commanded the 1st New York Battery.

[19] Major General A. A. Humphreys was Chief of Staff for Meade.

—Reported to Gen. W. in presence of Gen. M. (Lost all my notes as I rode).

12 M. heavy picket firing & art[y].

May 10
"5 P.M.

McCartny, Cowan, Rhodes[20] opened lively with their batteries—Russell with 1st Div, Vermont Brig.[21] & some other picked troops of Neill's massed to left & front of Cowan & McC. to attack—(postponed from 5 to 6 P.M. owing to enemy's having attacked Hancock & driven a Div[n]—they were repulsed by another Div[n]—Warren sent word to delay & I took it to Gen. Russell—) From 5.55 to 6.5½ batteries firing hell bent—At 6.5½ (now) they cease—Attack begins now 6.35—6.50 prisoners are & have been coming in with great rapidity—6.53 Tyler[22] comes for 2 Regts" The above in " " was noted at McCartny's Batty—at the times indicated, yesterday (10th) afternoon on back of my map—

The attack was on the front of a work perpendicular to ours & Russell says very carefully finished, high as a man's head & loopholes at top. The attacking party was disposed by Russell and led by Upton[23]—moved at *arms*

[20] Captain William B. Rhodes commanded Battery E of the 1st Rhode Island Artillery.

[21] The 2nd Brigade of the 2nd Division, Sixth Corps, was commanded by Colonel Lewis A. Grant.

[22] Perhaps Captain Mason W. Tyler, 37th Regiment Massachusetts Volunteers. See Mason Whiting Tyler, *Recollections of the Civil War* (New York, 1912), pp. 168-169.

[23] Colonel Upton was promoted to Brigadier General by Grant immediately after this assault.

a port slap into the works without firing a shot & took the whole first line (The very troops that stampeded Seymour's Brig. the other night)[24] to number of 950— Our loss in killed & wounded was heavy and a brilliant magnificent charge made useless except locally by entire failure of promised cooperation—Burnside didn't attack, nobody did anything to speak of except 6th Corps—

May 11

10:35 A.M.—our Art^y opens. Enemy reported moving towards our right—reported moving back, & again to right—

Mott was drawn in at daylight Hayden conducted him—I pleaded off (this was night of May 10th) not being confident that I could keep the road. M. was put in rear of our left—

The night of the 11th Hancock passed us en route for his attack of 12th & stopped at the Gen^{ls} tent (where Hayden & I were sleeping also) for directions as to the way—

Sheridan sends word he has cut Lee's communications & destroyed supplies—

[24] In the Wilderness, Seymour's Brigade had been disordered by General John B. Gordon's Brigade. (See *supra*, p. 106.) Upton's attack, here described, seems in fact to have been against Doles's Brigade.

Hq. 6 Corps
10.23 A.M. May 11. 64

Dear Mother

    I have written every chance I had—so far all right—
fighting every day—shan't try to tell particulars till I
can write at leisure—Just think of it—Today is the 7th
day we have fought, not pitched battles all the time of
course, but averaging a loss I guess of 3000 (three thousand) a day at least—

My love to all
Goodbye
O W H, Jr

T. Lyman[1]
Dalton[2] } O. K.

Whit. away with body of Gen. S.

[DIARY]

☞These notes made in this book at the times noted.

May 12—Foggy—{ Rain &
was soaked

---

[1] Lieutenant Colonel Theodore Lyman was Volunteer A.D.C. on the
staff of General Meade. His account of the Battles of the Wilderness
and Spottsylvania are found in *Meade's Headquarters, 1863-1865, Letters
of Colonel Theodore Lyman* (George R. Agassiz, ed.), (Boston, 1922),
pp. 85-117.

[2] Probably Major Edward B. Dalton.

Hancock having moved from our right to left of 6th C. (betw. it & Burnside) during the night—our guns opened at about 4.30 am,* in about a quarter hour we heard Hancock's shouts going in—Hard fighting—Now, 5.14 am, it is pretty quiet—that is doesn't sound like more than picket fire—No firing on front of 5th C. (now right of line) nor apparently by 6th C. Hancock's firing is where I have noted Gen. Mott 3 pp. back, [*supra* p. 110] in front of our line—A.M. 5.20 a little brisker—a shell or 2 round our H.Q. Firing sounds dull in fog—5.45. dispatch fr. Hancock that he had taken 2nd line of enemy's works had captured many prisoners and was pressing forward rapidly—

(Next note on the field 2.15 P.M.)

The enemy's last attack ceased 1.45 Whether they will try it again is a question—

7 P.M. They did try again & in brief All day we have been fighting & are banging away still—bullets are now whistling round these H.Q. & meanwhile a flock of little chickens are peeping & cheeping—their mother no doubt being in the belly of some soldier. The H.Q. where I write (Hancock, Wright, Barlow, Birney[1] et al.) are at a house in a direction   [2] from Mott's H.Q. (p. 8) [*supra* p. 110] our new line—

* Gen. Barlow[a] says attacked at 4.10—

[a] Brigadier General Francis C. Barlow, commanding 1st Division in Hancock's Second Corps.

[1] Major General David B. Birney, commanding the 3rd Division in Second Corps.

[2] Blank space in the original.

The firing had not ceased at 2 AM when I turned in—
In Brief Hancock did on a large scale what Mott was
intended to do 10th inst. He attacked in two lines of
battalions in mass—captured 3 generals,[3] many (   ) [4]
colors Over 3000 men & 18 or 22 guns. It was Johnson's Div. & he was taken. After the first success we did
not advance further during the day—The most stub-
born fighting was at a point of woods in front of Hancock's H.Q. & thither I had to ride between 11 & 2 P.M.
& put in a Regt (10th N. J.) [5] couldn't find Russell to
whom I was to report. Burnside who attacked on H's
left didn't make much. he is a d'd humbug—Warren
who is a ditto did about the same—We finally found a
new line facing down towards our old left & about perpendicular to the old front. In the morn'g went to Gen.
Meade for troops from Warren—Meade not only
wouldn't send any but stopped a Brig. wh. had started
—I think this was a mistake & that he should have
slapped in all he could spare on Hancock's front—I
think Warren represented himself harder pressed than
he was—The Gen[l] (W.) was hit in leg quite painfully
with a piece of shell not wounded however—We were
all under fire all day—
At "the angle" in a space of 12 by 15 ft between

[3] In fact two general officers were captured in this famous assault on
the Salient or Bloody Angle: Major General Edward Johnson and
Brigadier General George H. Steuart.
[4] Blank space in the original.
[5] This Regiment was part of the 1st Brigade of the 1st Division.

two traverses Col. Penrose[6] told Kent[7] he counted 150 bodies—

May 13—

7 A.M. The enemy has fallen back, we don't yet know how far—(They fell back very little) Day spent in straightening out Corps, burying dead, strengthening lines, &c.

In the corner of woods referred to yesterday the dead of both sides lay piled in the trenches 5 or 6 deep—wounded often writhing under superincumbent dead—The trees were in slivers from the constant peppering of bullets. *The losses of our Corps in these nine days are (10547) ten thousand five hundred & forty seven! Of which there is not a large proportion of missing—(This not counting Art[y] Brig. losses)

The enemy tried to press in our left picket towards evening—Orders to march to the left—either following or by parallel road with 5th C. I was sent to find road by wh. Warren would move—It was dark & raining & I got well turned round but found the head of the column—Ayres[8] (Griffin's Div.) & McKenzie[9]—They

* Afterwards reduced by return of stragglers &c to between nine & ten thousand—

[6] Colonel William H. Penrose commanded the New Jersey 1st Brigade in the 1st Division of Sixth Corps.

[7] Presumably Lieutenant Colonel J. Ford Kent, Inspector General of Sixth Corps.

[8] Brigadier General Romeyn B. Ayres commanded the 1st Brigade in the 1st Division of Sixth Corps.

[9] Probably Lieutenant Ranald S. Mackenzie of the Engineers.

marched by Hancock's H.Q. of 13th (Mott's) We had
to follow them late & had a terribly tiresome time Arrived at destination too late to surprise & turn enemy's
Right—

May 14. Made Beverly house about 5½ A.M. Gen.
Meade & Staff on the portico—got a little grub and felt
better
8.30 A.M. 300 of our infantry attacked a little house
to our left & front on a road—It was held by Rebs with
a section of Art^y. Upton started out just before with his
Brig.
8.40 We seem to have gained the house. After 3 P.M.
Upton was attacked & driven—Gen. Meade and Wright
were there scyugling[10] and had to mizzle rapidly—our
losses were small—Col. Wiebecke[11] killed & stripped
by Rebs
We found 3 lines at Anderson's house & after shelling
with 2 battys went forward at sunset—Ayre's Brig. 5th
C. got the house first (the Ny R. stopping our skirmishers & lines for some time from its depth) Up very late
establishing new line—About midnight, after getting
lost for a windup, struck H.Q. & a good feed & sleep.
This day with the night march before it, the long fast-

[10] A slang word originated by the Union Army having "a variety and
contrariety" of meaning. See John Russell Bartlett, *Dictionary of Ameri-
canisms* (4th ed.; Boston, 1874), pp. 600-601.

[11] Lieutenant Colonel Charles Wiebecke of the 2nd Regiment, New
Jersey Volunteers.

ing, the much riding, the getting lost &c was one of the most fatiguing we have had—

May 15ᵗʰ

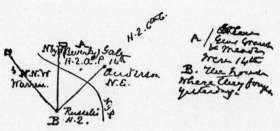

Morn'g—had a wash & good breakfast & rode out with the Genˡ to B.

All quiet during the day—Rainy—Orders towards sunset to be ready to attack at once—Enemy reported moving on Burnside's right & rear—Didn't have to move—

Butler reported to have taken outer works of Fᵗ Darling[12] & Averill to have cut E. Tenne. R.R. & destroyed depot at Dutton[13]—

[12] Major General Benjamin F. Butler's movement of the Army of the James up the James River had begun on May 4. On the 13th and 14th his forces succeeded in taking the outer defenses of Fort Darling at Drewry's Bluff, just south of Richmond. On the 16th, however, he was driven back to entrenchments between the fork of the James and Appomattox Rivers.

[13] Operations in the Shenandoah and Kanawha Valleys, under Major General Franz Sigel, had commenced on May 1. Between the 10th and 15th General William A. Averell had destroyed important portions of the East Tennessee and Virginia Railroad line near Wytheville, New River, and Christiansburg.

12. M.
May 15
H.Q. 6th Corps

All right
So far—
Direct to Capt O W H, Jr.
      A.D.C. *Maj.* Gen Wright
         Comdg 6th Corps
          W^n
           DC.
  Love to all
    O W H, Jr.

[DIARY]

May 16.

Had a good night's rest—

Below is a map of part of our present locality. Copied fr. Engineer Map—we came in (May 14th) by route indicated—formed 3 lines at F. Anderson & pushed for Meyers.* Ayre's Brig. 5th C. there first—see p. 14 [*supra* p. 119]

Sheridan reported to have licked & killed JEB Stuart & to have taken 2 guns fr. outer works of Richmond[1]

* Meyers H. is the one to wh. Upton and our whole line later advanced 14th

[1] These successes occurred on May 10.

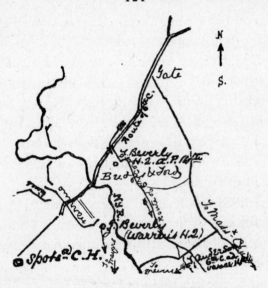

Now on way to rejoin us—good news also from Sher-man[2]—

May 16th 1864
H. Q. 6th Corps—

Dear Parents

Rec'd last night enclosed letters—Yesterday & to-day tolerably quiet, a quiet that you will easily believe was needed after the long series of collisions beginning on the 5th—Before you get this you will know how im-mense the butchers bill has been—And the labor has been incessant—I have not been & am not likely to be

[2] General Sherman's campaign from Chattanooga to Atlanta opened on May 6.

in the mood for writing details. I have kept brief notes in my diary wh. I hope you may see some day—Enough that these nearly two weeks have contained all of fatigue & horror that war can furnish—The advantage has been on our side but nothing decisive has occurred & the enemy is in front of us strongly intrenched—I doubt if the decisive battle is to be fought between here & Richmond—nearly every Regimental off— I knew or cared for is dead or wounded—

I have made up my mind to stay on the staff if possible till the end of the campaign & then if I am alive, I shall resign—I have felt for sometime that I didn't any longer believe in this being a duty & so I mean to leave at the end of the campaign as I said if I'm not killed before.[1] Remember I am now at H.Q. 6th C. & it is *Major Gen*[1] *W. Comdg*—

[1] Writing to Charles Eliot Norton on April 17, 1864, and expressing appreciation of Norton's article in the *North American Review* for April on St. Louis and Joinville, Holmes had said:

"I have long wanted to know more of Joinville's Chronicle than I did, but the story seems to come up most opportunely now when we need all the examples of chivalry to help us bind our rebellious desires to steadfastness in the Christian Crusade of the 19th century. If one didn't believe that this war was such a crusade, in the cause of the whole civilized world, it would be hard indeed to keep the hand to the sword; and one who is rather compelled unwillingly to the work by abstract conviction than borne along on the flood of some passionate enthusiasm, must feel his ardor rekindled by stories like this. . . . In all probability from what I hear of the filling up of the Regt. I shall soon be mustered in for a new term of service as Lt. Col. of the 20th and so with double reason I am thankful to read of the great dead who have 'stood in the evil day.' No—it will not do to leave Palestine yet." The original of this letter is in the possession of the Houghton Library, Harvard University and is reprinted here with the University's permission.

The duties & thoughts of the field are of such a
nature that one cannot at the same time keep home, parents and such thoughts as they suggest in his mind at the
same time as a reality—Can hardly indeed remember
their existence—and this too just after the intense yearn-
ing which immediately precedes a campaign Still your
letters are the one pleasure & you know my love

Your Aff. Son
O W H Jr

[DIARY]

May 17.

11 A.M. A. fork in road [1] B ravine & stream*

C. house & rebels Cav^y videttes stopped here
from 11 A.M. to 1 P.M.

D. road here 45° N. of W. E F 780 ft.

F.   "   "   40° " " "

G. pines stop & a more open oak wood
begins.

FG. over 900 ft. GH 500 H. 2.15 P.M.

HI. Ab^t 500 ft. Russell's pickets advanced &
run along the road fr.   [2] to angle I (obtuse)
The original road at I red clay & very muddy.
Shooting (a dozen shots) in front ab^t 3.10 P.M.

*AE ab^t 1/2 or 3/4 m. From F to H belt of woods of
only ab^t 20 ft on R. of road.

[1] See map, next page.
[2] Blank space in the original.

This country is hilly—More shooting later—Our
advance ceased ab^t 300 yds beyond the ridge—
a a The line from Carter H. to road is that of Ricketts
& Neill taken up on 19th.

Reconnoissance
3d V^t & 10th Mass Infty Col. Seaver[3]

[3] On the 16th Colonel Thomas O. Seaver of the 3rd Regiment Vermont Volunteers, commanding his own Regiment and the 10th Massachusetts, made a reconnaissance towards Spottsylvania Court House.

May 18ᵗʰ (Notes at times indicated)

Marched back to Right following 2nd C. to Landrum House—Hancock had been moving to our left & enemy concentrating on his Right so we try to get him by a reverse movement. We were to attack at 4 A.M.[4]—delayed—1st shots at 4.30 A.M. 4.39 (35?)* Hancock orders attack—our 3d Div.[5] not yet formed—5.37 A.M. in our earthworks in front of Lᵐ'ˢ. Rebel shell & roundshot lively—One of our Battys close to us replying. 5.56 A narrow escape—shell burst in the face of the Gen. & rest of us, stinging all, hurting none. 7½ A.M. Gen. Ricketts, ESE, WNW, line crosses morass. Vᵗ Brig log works N.N.E. SSW

5.15 P.M. We are back at Anderson's & I have had a bath a drink & a dinner—I was nearly dead beat & am now quite well—

The attack (we will call it a reconnoissance) was a failure—Took their rifle pits but stuck at main works—

Our (6th C's) last attempt was to swing forward our right (Ricketts) & I took the order to try it if practicable (See above, 7½ AM) but he said it was threatened & he couldn't do it. There were sharpshooters of the enemy in the open on his right & rear, as I experi-

* 4.35 by Capt.   ᵃ watch of Hancᵏ'ˢ staff—

ᵃ This space is blank in the original.
[4] This assault of the 18th was directed again on the Salient at Spottsylvania.
[5] Commanded by General Ricketts.

enced—Then Gen. W. sent me with a dispatch to Humphreys that he had tried all & found no weak point & I took back an order (8.56 A.M.) to withdraw beginning on Right & by a covered road near Burnside's picket line. I hear of Capts Curtis[6] (comfortably) & Kelliher[7] (very severely) hurt in our Regt. today—The whole ground stunk horribly with dead men & horses of previous fight —At Army H.Q. (8.50 A.M.) Cadwalader[8] gave me a swallow of brandy & Lyman 2 hardtack & some guava wh. greatly revived me after riding all yesterday, last night & this morn'g & having had nothing since dinner yesterday & no sleep—

We got back about 2 P.M. It was 1.15 just before we got to Meyers (H.Q. 1st & 3d Div. 17th) Letters fr. Mother, A. H. & F. B. D.

May 19.

Up at about 3 A.M. Some change—I think only in line of our works, but it is not yet developed—to our left—went first to Meyers H. then out by road marked p. 17. [*supra* p. 124] then out about to K (same map) our pickets having been advanced—then struck off to right along picket line, as I thought, to find out, by the Gen[ls] order, where the left of our new line would be—I succeeded in getting entirely lost—& brought up by good luck in one of Warren's rifle pits having just been head-

---

[6] Captain Arthur R. Curtis, commanding Company I.
[7] Captain John Kelliher, commanding Company C.
[8] Captain Charles E. Cadwalader was on General Meade's staff.

ing for the enemy's wh. were within a gunshot. After further wanderings and fetching up on Meyers H. en route I found the Genl some way back on road—8.10 A.M. about quarter hour ago rode along Neill & Ricketts new front to Carter house (Ricketts left.)

Burnside takes position on our left.

Hancock said to be at Anderson's Mill & also said to be Guinea's St^a

In the ev'g there was firing to Warren's right & rear (W. is now on right of the army)—I hear nothing very definite this morn'g (20th) but the enemy captured 20 or 30 of our teams wh. were retaken by Corcoran's Legion unhurt[9]—Tyler's Div^n (new troops) hefty Art^y (now serving as Inft^y) are said to have taken 400 prisoners—Birney's Div^n wh. was marching t'other way turned right about & went in—Ewell's Corps[10] was engaged—They say they are about used up with marching back & forward &c—

Russell's (1st Div.) & Wheaton's Brig.[11] moved at night to the right to relieve the 2^d Corps.

Saw Gen. Burnside who remembered our interview at the 5th Av^e Hotel just after my wound at Ball's Bluff —He desired his regards to the governor of course[12]—

[9] On May 17 Brigadier General R. O. Tyler, commanding the Corcoran Legion and heavy artillery units serving as infantry, had joined the Second Corps.

[10] Lieutenant General R. S. Ewell commanded the Second Army Corps of the Army of Northern Virginia.

[11] Brigadier General Frank Wheaton commanded the 1st Brigade in the 2nd Division (Getty's) of the Sixth Corps.

[12] Following this entry the rough beginning of a sketch map appears.

May 20th

Out after breakfast to see (with Haydn) that Ricketts & Neill made a continuous 1st line & nearly continuous 2^d & that Russell & Wheaton were replaced—
(R. & W. moved off to right last night.)

Then rode with Gen. W. & Gen. Burnside first &
Gen. Meade later, round our line & that of B. & of Warren—establishing new line—our right to be at Meyers
House, Warren to go off somewhere & B.'s line & ours
to be in the general direction of Meyers & Quisenberry
in rear of pres^t one—I had a fatiguing day, though most
of the staff hadn't much to do. Letter from Mother
dated 17th wrote F B D.

Ev'g—rather much whiskey and a very pleasant
time listening to Dr. Oehlenschlager's[13] singing & others.
It was delightful & a singular contrast to troops marching by, working parties &c &c—

I. A. & N. Journ. p. 658.[14]

May 21—

Up at 4 A.M. relieving Farrar in the succession of
Order [sic] sent out, somewhat uselessly, to be pres^t
during the night at the making of the new line of earth
works—After breakfast rode with the Gen. & then to
Warren's H.Q. to find out how he would move—He
takes road on other side, (left), of Ny R.
We withdrew to new line when W.'s troops are all out

---

[13] Not identified.
[14] The *Army and Navy Journal* for Saturday, May 28, 1864 (I, 658)
carried an account of the campaign in Virginia from May 17 to May 24.

of the way—W. promised to notify us when he withdrew his pickets—also informed me that he sh^d withdraw his left Brig. at once to rejoin its Div^n—Saw Barnard,[15] Nathan Appleton[16] & Johnny Bigelow[17] at the head of his Batty (the last time I saw him was at White-Oak Swamp his Batty going full galop—) They fired a few shots at Warren's trains or troops as I was returning —Ev'g brisk attack on our skirmishers & our Battys opened. Ev'g begun to move towards Guinea Br. after Burnside—At a little before 2 A.M. I was sent to H.Q. A.P. wh. I reached with some difficulty at about 4½ a. m. to report that owing to some hitch in the trains ahead (Burnside's I believe) our last ambulances & guns had done no more than move into the road & suggest that the Cav^y wh. Gen. Wright had ordered to start off & report to H. Q. A. P. at 12 sh^d be sent back to cover our right & rear—

May 22.

They (Young[18] Humphreys & Co) treated me very hospitably at H. Q. A. P. and gave me wash & food— and while waiting for a return dispatch I got a little sleep —Rode up and down the road crowded with wagons artillery & troops till I had enough of it—This forenoon

[15] Probably Captain George M. Barnard, Jr., of the 18th Regiment Massachusetts Volunteers, which constituted a part of the 3rd Brigade, 1st Division of Fifth Corps.

[16] Second Lieutenant Nathan Appleton of the 5th Battery (Battery E) of the Massachusetts Light Artillery.

[17] Captain John Bigelow, commanding the 9th Battery, Massachusetts Light Artillery.

[18] Not identified.

H. Q. A. P. at Motley's house "Molloy" on map—Hancock today is at Milford's St[a]

We march via Motley Stannards marsh & Catletts Houses (am at the latter now (1.50 P.M.) and have heard for some time lively cannonado to the S.W.) halted at "Madison's (ordinary)" within a mile or so of telegraph road—Warren ahead on telegraph road—Burnside somewhere in rear—

May 23.

Orders to move sent out at 7 A.M.[19] Moved at about 7½—Stopped at Plippo's[20] house where were 2 or 3 wounded Rebs Warren's H.Q. last night—12 M. at Mrs. Allen's about a mile from Dr. Plippo—It is reported that Ewell foll[d] by Longstreet—begun to pass here Saturday night & were passing yesterday & that the head of Warren's column came up about half an hour after.

The straggling & marauding have become a great evil—Families are robbed and houses burned constantly by ruffians, chiefly, I suspect, noncombatants who move along the outskirts of the column.

This day was very fatiguing—When head of column reached Goldensville I galloped on with the General to Mt. Carmel Church & then back & then rode at

[19] This movement to the South took the Army of the Potomac across the North Anna, Pamunkey, Chickahominy, and James Rivers, across the battlefields of the Seven Days, and led it, after Cold Harbor, to Petersburg.

[20] This house has also been designated as Flipper's House and Flippo's House.

head of column to Church again & then back to tail of column &c. &c—trains parked at Church; our H.Q. at Jericho ford (N. Anna R.) very little sleep at night—our wagons didn't come up till late & we didn't arrive ourselves till well after dark—I got to H.Q. about 10 P.M.

May 24.

A nasty hot dusty day devoted to what was called rest but wasn't—Morn'g 2nd and 1st Div[s] crossed the river[21]—Warren did well by us about crossing—He sent word the night before, he didn't need us, and again this morn'g when Meade w[d] have hurried us across in the night & disorganized the Corps into stragglers—Hancock shooting with Artillery all day—

Ev'g severe lightning & thunder just as we changed our H.Q. across the ford.

May 25

This morn'g we advanced by Noel's St[n] in direction SE by E formed line of battle Neill on left Russell R. Ricketts in rear with trains—Warren (Griffin) on our left 2 guns at 12 m. from us—at some Cav[y]—sh[d] not have been fired—a queer contrast with the piano & singing from wh. a party of us were started out—

Day spent in establishing the line. Russell not finally est[d] till ev'g—owing to an aide of Gen. Grant setting the Div[n] destroying the R. R. (V[a] Central) Ricketts in a sort of echelon to Right & rear—Neill's left running

[21] The North Anna

S.E. joined Warren (5th C.) at about a right angle the latter running N.E (fr. right to left) The line is along Little R. Burnside is not across the N. Anna—Hancock is, on left of B. At night our trains recrossed the N. Anna—

May 26—

Russell's Div. & the Cav[y] ordered to move down the other bank (left) of the Anna & cross the Pamunkey at Hanover Town—

Day quiet—Rode with the Gen[l] to Warren's H.Q. At dark the rest of the Corps moved—a thunder storm in the morn'g & another in the ev'g made the first several miles of the road horrible—At daybreak struck Chesterfield

May 27

All day on road—Camped at ev'g in beautiful country (in line) on a ridge with a broad river bottom in front & below us—

May 28—

A march of about 4½ m. and then crossed the Pamunkey[22] as soon as the pontoon br. (5 boats 125 ft.) was done—Taylor's Ford—Found Sheridan & Torbert's Div[n] Cav[y] on t'other side—saw Harry Winsor[23] & had a good talk—

[22] At a point four miles above Hanover Town.
[23] Presumably Lieutenant Henry Winsor, who had been temporarily in the class of 1860 at Harvard, and who was at this time in the 6th Pennsylvania Volunteer Cavalry, part of General Torbert's Division of the Cavalry Corps.

May 29 Saw Hayward & Perry[24]—P. gave
        me a letter from C. I. Dehon[25]
A stunning night's rest—The loveliest morning we
have had Between 10 & 11 A.M. went out to Jones H.
to find road for part of Russell's Column to Hanover
C. H. plantation road leading out fr. Grant's line (V^t
Brig.) by Jones then turning to R. into woods—Went
back & reported to Gen. W. & Meade & then forward
with column (McMahon[26] McClellan[27] Col. Tomkins[28]
&c. there—) About a mile fr. Jones struck cav^y videttes
—(rebels)—McMahon & I sitting at edge of woods at
1.18 P.M. close together on horseback, a stray shot
struck McM.'s horse in the breast—another hit a man
in column at 1.30—

Later—About an hour before sunset the Genl gave
me a dispatch to Russell[29] & told me not to spare my

[24] Presumably John G. Perry, assistant to Surgeon Nathan Hayward
of the 20th Regiment.
[25] Caroline Inches Dehon, later Mrs. Adams Sherman Hill, was the
sister of Holmes's college classmate Arthur Dehon, who, while A.D.C. to
General Meade, had been killed at Fredericksburg and of whom Holmes
wrote a biographical sketch in the *Harvard Memorial Biographies*
(Cambridge, 1866), II, 233.
[26] Probably Lieutenant Colonel Martin T. McMahon, Assistant Adjutant General, Sixth Corps.
[27] Presumably Captain Arthur McClellan, brother of General McClellan, who served on General Wright's staff.
[28] Presumably Colonel Charles H. Tompkins, Chief of Artillery, Sixth
Corps.
[29] General Russell's Division led the Sixth Corps in the reconnaissance which that Corps, together with the Second and Fifth Corps,
had been ordered to make on the 29th. His advance was towards Hanover Court House from its position south of the Pamunkey on the River
Road at Crump's Creek.

horse—when I turned fr. plantation road into Lane Upton's boyscout came riding along back full tilt & sung
out to me not to go on, he had been fired at by 2 reb.
cav^y. Dilemma—concluded must go on—picked up a
straggler (inft^y), an unarmed man on a mule a sick officer & the boy & was starting when I saw 3 or 4 cav^y
foragers—got them & sent back rest except Upton's boy
whose head is level—trot to place where boy was shot
at—then gallop to where the road bends to right—bang
—whiz—"Halt" "Surrender" fr. about 20 Rebs. in line
—I thought it was a mistake & they were friends & begun to pull up but saw the gray jackets & clapped the
spurs to my horse—much shooting—presently a fellow
comes down the road "Surrender" he hadn't got his
carbine quite unslung & I put my pistol to his breast &
pulled trigger—missed fire—then he & others on right
of road do shooting I lying along the side of horse
Comanche fashion—2 of my men got through with
me—I soon struck pickets & Duffy[30] saw Russell & returned on other road with answer

[30] Probably Lieutenant Colonel James N. Duffy, Acting Inspector-
General of Russell's 1st Division. A rough sketch of the terrain of this
incident, substantially identical with that reproduced in the letter of
May 30, 1864 (*infra*, p. 137), is omitted.

May 30th 64
4.12 P.M.

Dear Parents

Wrote to Anna[1] this morn'g—who may send to you—imprimis rec^d y'r letters of 21st 22^d the latter fr. dad, stupid—I wish you'd take the trouble to read my letters before answering—I am sure I cannot have conveyed the idea, rightfully,[2] that I intended resigning before the campaign was over (i.e. next winter just near the end of my term of service)—then I probably shall for reasons satisfactory to myself—I must say I dislike such a misunderstanding, so discreditable to my feeling of soldierly honor, when I don't believe there was a necessity for it—I shall stay on the staff and wish you'd notify the Governor to commission new field officers to the 20th I waive promotion—I am convinced from my late experience that if I can stand the wear & tear (body & mind) of regimental duty that it is a greater strain on both than I am called on to endure—If I am satisfied I don't really see that anyone else has a call to be otherwise—I talked with Hayward the mentor of the Regt & told him my views on the matter—I am not the same man (may not have quite the same ideas) & certainly am not so elastic as I was and I *will not acknowledge the same claims upon me under those circumstances* that existed formerly—a day & a half have passed

[1] Presumably Anna Hallowell, sister of Norwood Penrose Hallowell.
[2] Presumably in his letter of May 16, *supra*, p. 121.

since I wrote last word—it is quarter to 12 between
May 31. & June 1 I have just been riding through black
woods after some H^{d}Qrs—and we are going to have
another of those killing night marches as soon as we can
start out of a country worse than the wilderness if possible[3]—I have hardly known what a good night's sleep
was since the campaign opened—constantly having, as
tonight, to be up all night—

The afternoon of the 29th I had my narrowest escape—Dispatch to carry—important—don't spare y'r
horse—gallop—1 mile—small boy (one well known as
Col. Upton's scout) retreating at a run—reports fired at
2 reb. cav^y—looked round for forces—one straggler
(infty) one (unarmed) man on mule, one sick officer—
& boy—I spy 4 of our cav^y foraging dismiss former
forces & order them with me—trot—when boy was shot
at gallop—bend in road—woods cease—bang—bang—
whiz—whiz—about 20 reb^s in line—"Halt. Surrender"
I pulled up & sung out "friends" deceived by number &
darkness of their clothes—They keep on shooting then
I saw & put in licks for straight ahead—Anon a fellow
comes riding down the road—I think I'll gobble him—
he to me "Halt Surrender" I see others on R. of road
—he is unslinging his carbine as I get to him, I put my
pistol to his breast & pull—enclosed cap snaps—then

[3] On the 30th the Sixth Corps had been directed to move across the
tangled and swampy terrain between Hanover Court House and the
Totopotomoy where General Hancock's Second Corps was in need of
reinforcement.

SIXTH CORPS HEADQUARTERS AT COLD HARBOR, JUNE 1, 1864

I run the gauntlet—bang—whiz—Halt—Surrender lying along the neck of my horse—Got my dispatch

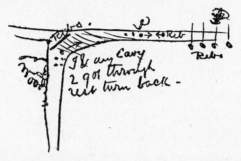

through & return in triumph to find myself given over
for lost—[4]

Love to all
Afftly
O W H, Jr.

[DIARY]

May 30—Babnew[1] orderly
    Letters fr. Mother & father (21st, 22d) & A. H.
22ᵈ—Very hard day—

May 31.
    Morn'g on the line—Pickets advanced as far as pos-
sible—

[4] On the back of the envelope was written the following:
"O.K. June 2ᵈ ev.g Send me good lead pencil—Whit. arrived yesterday with late letters Write as often as poss. It is still kill—kill—all the
time—"

[1] Not identified.

Then went with Franklin[2] to look out roads in rear of Warren[3]—via Hawes Shops Midnight moved[4] —Another nasty night—dust horrible—

June 1st.

Moved to Cold (Coal) Harbor via Old Church— One of the most miserable days—heat & dust—no breakfast—nearly dropping from my saddle with fatigue—Cav[y] fight at C. H. in morn'g— About 5 ½ P.M. we attacked—Gen. (Baldie) Smith[5] on our right swung forward—we foll'g the movement— the prisoners taken—several hundred—were fr. Beauregard[6] & McLaws[7] Div. of Longstreet— Mem. Losses up to today 9332—of wh. 1429 missing—

June 2[d]

This morn'g the Cav[y] is to reconnoitre to Sumner's Upper Bridge—Our orders are to attack when Hancock arrives in position & has part of his force in supporting position—

Attack postponed to 5 P.M. & then 4 tomorrow A.M. Today gave feed and rum first to Gen. Smith &

[2] Presumably Captain W. S. Franklin, Commissary of Musters, Sixth Corps.

[3] General Warren's Fifth Corps had crossed the Totopotomoy on the 30th and was advancing along the Shady Grove Church road towards Richmond.

[4] To support General Sheridan at Cold Harbor.

[5] Major General William F. Smith's Eighteenth Corps had arrived at White House on the 31st and had marched up the south bank of the Pamunkey, reaching the front lines near Cold Harbor on the 1st.

[6] General P. G. T. Beauregard's main force was at Petersburg and Bermuda Hundred.

[7] General Lafayette McLaws was in General Longstreet's Corps.

Staff—then Hancock Gibbon[8] & Staff then Meade, Grant & Staffs & we are cleaned out—
Paid Henry[9] for May $15.

June 3ᵈ

Ordered to attack at 4 A.M.; did, a little later, it being a rainy morning[10]—The soldiers call these things "Morning reports" & they have a sort of mush of hard tack wh. they call "Son of a b—h"—hard firing a good deal of the morning Now 12.15 M. shooting somewhat less—These H.Q. (3ᵈ Div.) under a lively fire all the time—This divⁿ has gone forward as far as possible the 1st Divⁿ being in rear on the left (owing to halt of 2d C. on left of it) and Gen. Neill[11] having halted on right. The left of 3ᵈ Div. being badly enfiladed in new position it was refused a little by order of Gen. Ricketts (Gen. W. consenting)

June 4

Our H.Q. not changed[12]—Sent to Ricketts front in the morn'g—Sharpshooters put a bullet wherever you show a head—Day quiet—Row at night[13]—

[8] Brigadier General John Gibbon commanded the 2nd Division in the Second Corps (Hancock's).

[9] Probably Holmes's orderly.

[10] This was the engagement at New Cold Harbor, one mile west of Cold Harbor.

[11] The 2nd Division, previously under the command of General Getty, was now commanded by Brigadier General Thomas H. Neill.

[12] Between June 4 and June 12 the Army of the Potomac remained in its advance positions under constant fire but without major assaults against the Confederates who were on the left bank of the Chickahominy.

[13] On the inside of the back cover of the Diary appears the following

June 5.

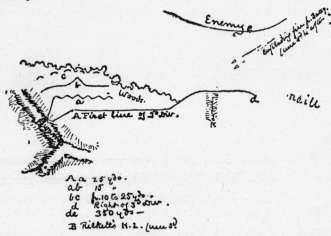

To front of 3d Div. & along the lines—sketched above—
Distances as given by Officers there. I thought them generally less—Row at night—

...12 M. June 5......., 1864

Dear Parents
    Rec'd a no. of delightful letters from you—Also cigars by Whittier—*Many* thanks—A thousand loving thoughts this Sunday Morng—The earlier part of wh. has been spent on the front line of works drawing them & dodging bullets—

---

item: "Memorandum—My meerschaum to Major Whittier if I am killed—June 4ᵗʰ O W Holmes Jr."

I just heard of the mails as it was going—Goodbye
Love to all—Thank Lilly Jackson[1] for a very
kind letter & explain that I am unable to answer it in
these days—

Your Affectionate
O W H Jr

[DIARY]

June 6th

Mail goes every day now—Haven't noted letters
written or rec^d—day beautiful & quiet till afternoon—
our right (Burnside & part of Smith) having been swung
back so as to make almost a semicircle the enemy
opened with a section taking us almost if not quite in
reverse & rather bothering our H.Q. There was much
stampeding of wagons, bands, hospital men & other noncombatants—

H.Q. 6th Corps
June 7/64

Dear Mother

Here goes for the luxury of writing a decent looking letter, using the cigar box which father sent me as a

[1] Elizabeth Cabot Jackson, Holmes's cousin, who subsequently married
Henry Winsor.

desk—that is I will write if the enemy will give me time and not go pitching shell & roundshot round our H.Q. as they have been doing earlier this morn'g, and if they will keep decently quiet on the front line of works. A cheerful place the latter, by the way, to be sent to after breakfast to inspect & report on progress—You show your nose anywhere and sizzle come the bullets at it in less than the twinkling of a bedpost—and they shoot pretty well on both sides now. However I am so much safer than any inft^y officer that I don't grumble but also feel that I am earning less honor though learning much more—

But fortunately I have a jewel in the head of this campaign in the shape of my adventure of Sunday week ago—For let me tell you what I wouldn't before as I was a little irritated, that, although I am not aware of the General's knowing the particulars, the staff to whom I spun my yarn intimated that they thought it rather a gallant thing, & it was I think myself to get the order through & not knock under or turn back—

These days of comparative rest though constant loss allow my thoughts to turn longingly & lovingly homeward again—which they couldn't—as I told you— in the wear and tear of alternate march and fight.

The campaign has been most terrible yet believe me I was not demoralized when I announced my intention to leave the service next winter if I lived so long— I started in this thing a boy I am now a man and I have

been coming to the conclusion for the last six months
that my duty has changed—

I can do a disagreeable thing or face a great danger
coolly enough when I *know* it is a duty—but a doubt
demoralizes me as it does any nervous man—and now
I honestly think the duty of fighting has ceased for me—
ceased because I have laboriously and with much suffer-
ing of mind and body *earned* the right which I denied
Willy Everett[1] to decide for myself how I can best do
my duty to myself to the country and, if you choose,
to God—

I believe that Governor Andrew understands my
determination to waive promotion—please be sure he
does so—The ostensible and sufficient reason is my hon-
est belief that I cannot now endure the labors & hardships of the line[2]—Nothing further need be told
abroad—

I hope that this will meet your approbation—you
are so sure to be right—at all events I have tried to decide conscientiously & I have decided—

[1] Presumably William Everett, of the Harvard Class of 1859, who
spent the Civil War studying in England.

[2] Writing to his friend Agnes Pomeroy of Pittsfield on June 21, 1864,
Holmes said:
"Do you know I shall never wear the "20" again? . . . I have written the
Governor that I waive promotion. I find myself too weak from previous campaigns to do the duties of an officer of the line properly. Our
medical director (6th C) told me the other day that I was not keeping
up by the strength of my constitution now but by the stimulus of this
constant pressure to which we have been subjected." This letter is
quoted by kind permission of Miss Edith Bartlett of Pittsfield, daughter
of General Bartlett and Agnes (Pomeroy) Bartlett.

If you know Carrie Dehons direction please let Amelia write a note & thank her for a very kind note wh. I recᵈ long after it was written & explain the difficulty of answering it in person—

Love, Love, Love to all of you—Why don't F. McG write? I long for a letter from her

Recᵈ Amelia's letter last night—I wish she'd write often—and that Ned would also sling ink—

Your loving
O W Holmes, Jr.

[DIARY]

June 7—

Musketry as usual at night (about 1 A.M.) & about 3 waked by that stinking battery again—Sent to Russell to inquire progress—

June 8–9, 10, 11

In camp—nothing especial except running a new line of earthworks in rear of old ones by wh. to fall back—

June 12.

Morn'g orders to move at ev'g[1]—

At midnight started, having fallen back to 2nd line of works just after sunset—At Hopkins' Mill road was

[1] The movement was to Wilcox's Landing, just below Charles City Court House, where the crossing of the James River was to be effected.

found to be impassible except for infantry—so arty &
all the Wheels went by Prospect Ch— Morn'g our
H.Q. got breakfast near the Richm^d & York Riv. R.R.
June 13th A hard day's march Crossed Chickahominy
at Soan's [*sic*]² bridge—an old canal is now the main
channel here (bridged with only 2 pontons) & the original bed only required a single ponton—Camped for the
night just across the Riv. 9th C. didn't cross—we
marched fastest & arrived first—

June 14th
Marched to neighborhood of Ch. City C. H.³ I ac-
companied Gen. Russell—Our H.Q. at a house (Chris-
tians) with the finest bush of white roses on the porch
I ever saw—all in bloom—

June 15th
This morn'g the line was a little changed—The Corps
is to cover all the crossing⁴—The line about E. & W.
facing N. H.Q. at another beautiful house.

June 16.
Morn'g Moved our H.Q. to banks of James R. and
expected to wait till everything had crossed—but orders
came in afternoon for 1st & 3d Div^ns to go by transport
and 2nd Div^n & Artillery by the pontoon br. and road to

---

² The crossing appears to have been at what is generally known as
Jones's Bridge.
³ Charles City Court House
⁴ The 101 pontoon bridges, over which the Army crossed the James,
were located a short distance below Windmill Point.

City P.t—H.Q. and H.Q. 3d Div. embarked on 1st boat —arriving at C^y P^t were ordered to Bermuda Hundreds vessels of light draught going to P^t of Rocks—Late at night made Butler's H.Q.[5] with one Brig. t'other landing at P. of R.[6]

June 20.[7]

Shelled severely early in morn'g—much rum—got tight—then went to right—

June 21.

Morn'g some good practice (& some poor, Schenkl ammunition bad) from 330 p^{dr} Parrots on the R. of our H.Q. at the batt^y wh. has annoyed us—could see shells strike the parapet & explode—

Evg ordered to left of the Army,[8] marched at nightfall & no sleep at all—

June 23—
Upton's brig. R. of 1st Div.[9]

[5] The Headquarters of General Butler's Army of the James was at Bermuda Hundreds. General W. F. Smith had reached that headquarters from Cold Harbor on the 14th, and on the 15th had opened his assault on the Petersburg entrenchments.

[6] Point of Rocks.

[7] The Sixth Corps was not substantially engaged in the Petersburg operations of June 17 and 18. The positions then gained by the Second, Fifth, and Ninth Corps were held without appreciable change until the close of the war. On the 19th the Sixth Corps crossed the Appomattox and rejoined the Army of the Potomac.

[8] On the 21st the Second and Sixth Corps moved across the Jerusalem Plank Road with a view to the taking of the Weldon Railroad line south of Petersburg.

[9] Colonel Upton's 2nd Brigade was in the 1st Division of the Sixth Corps.

N & S facing W. extreme R. 49th Pa. NE.[10] Jerseys[11]
E. 4th Brig. N.

6.15 P.M. The enemy has pushed our skirmish line hard
for an hour or so—some shots just now into our H.Q.
We have just sent for 2 Brig. to 2ᵈ C. & whatever else
they could send—The troops in the angle of the
crotchet on our left (picket line) (2ᵈ Div.) were
gobbled to extent of hundred—

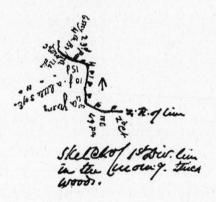

June 23ᵈ 7.10 am

Dear Mother

Another infernal nasty time—night before last the
Corps moved from right to left of Army—that night no
sleep—All day troops changing position—advancing retreating advancing again usual accompaniment of shoot-

[10] Of the 3rd Brigade of the 1st Division.
[11] 1st Brigade, 1st Division.

ing—A brigade of the 2d Div 2d Corps behaved badly yesterday & lost 4 guns the first guns ever taken from the Corps[1]—last up very late—a brief sleep on the floor of a house with all my harness on rose at 3 this a.m. for an attack wh. was ordered—So far there has been nothing but a little picket shooting

The Genl's going out Goodbye

Yr loving Son
W.

Recd father's letter of 19th

June 24th 64/

Dear Parents

Just the time I stopped my last letter to pres[t] moment a constant go—fighting—forward & back nothing of any account however except losing several hundred prisoners yesterday & 2[d] Corps losing the same & 4 guns day before—20th I hear ran like thunder[1]—

Father'd better not talk to me about opinions at home & here—On the staff one can form a far better opinion of the *particular campaign* than one at home—

It's true Smith says the niggers will fight—I heard

---

[1] This incident occurred when the enemy advanced between the Sixth and Second Corps and surprised the left flank of General Gibbon's 2nd Division.

[1] The remnants of the old 20th Regiment were in the 1st Brigade of General Gibbon's 2nd Division.

him.[2] Read Page's "(C.A.P.)" letters to Tribune—they are good—though he is a nasty toadying snob—like most correspondents[3] I hope you have kept or will secure some daily (newspaper) record of this campaign & also a pictorial (Harper) *Waud*[4] is quite a truthful draughtsman—

These last few days have been very bad—This morn'g I spent on the picket line it was being pushed forward—hot & nasty as Orcus—I think there is a kind of heroism in the endurance (Interrupted here to carry order to Gen Ricketts Comdg 3d Div 6th C to cut road in rear of line &c—R. of famous battery at 1st Bull Run wounded & prisoner Mrs. R—heroic—goes to see & comfort R. in jug & he is made Brig. Gen.) in the endurance I was going to say of the men—I tell you many a man has gone

[2] The 3rd Division of General William F. Smith's Eighteenth Corps, commanded by Brigadier General Edward W. Hinks, included two Brigades of Negro Troops which had played an important and gallant part in the Petersburg operations.

[3] Selected letters of Charles A. Page were later published in *Letters of a War Correspondent* (1899), edited by J. R. Gilmore. In his dispatch of July 20, 1864, Page, speaking of the departure of the 20th Regiment on expiration of its service, said of Holmes:

"Practically, the most important consideration is that so many trained and valuable officers are thus lost to the service. Of the Twentieth, Oliver Wendell Holmes, Jr. . . . was an officer. Captain Holmes served more than two years steadily and chivalrously as a line officer, was three times severely wounded, and in this campaign has been zealous and indefatigable as a member of the Sixth Corps staff, has always been conspicuously daring, and capably efficient, and he goes out of service because his regiment does, not because he would taste the sweets of home and Boston."—(*Id.* pp. 176-177.)

[4] Alfred R. Waud, artist for *Harper's Weekly.*

crazy since this campaign begun from the terrible pressure on mind & body—

I think the Army feels better than it might but theres no use in disguising that the feeling for McClellan has grown this campaign—I hope for success strongly before the end of the summer—but at what a cost & by & by the sickness will begin—I hope to pull through but don't know yet—

Afftly

Goodbye

O W H, Jr.

[DIARY]

June 24

On picket line all the morn'g—it was pushed forward again to near position of the 23^d—left well refused and front not quite so far advanced—

June 25.

Morn'g quiet in camp—hot as thunder—had a shave & shampoo—

July 1.

Morn'g changed H.Q. from Tucker's to a Field—Message from Gen. Meade for rough sketch of position of 6th C. Went out and made that on next page wh. I copied neatly and sent up—

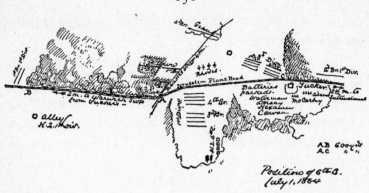

July 2^d

Moved back to the entrenchments—We have been at our old H.Q. ever since—I was with Getty—rear of column—very dusty—very hot[1]—

H.Q. 6th C.
July 8th 1864[1]

Dear Mammy

Prepare for a startler—Unless something unexpected happens I shall probably leave this army for home about the 17th! [2] The Regt. ceases to exist as a Regt and

---

[1] This is the last entry in the diary.

---

[1] The Sixth Corps between July 6 and July 9 began its hasty movement to Washington to meet Early's threat on the city from the north. Units of the Corps arrived just in time to repulse the attack at Fort Stevens on July 12. The Sixth Corps did not thereafter return to the Army of the Potomac and General Wright assumed a new command in the Shenandoah Campaign.

[2] The envelope, in the handwriting of Holmes's mother, indicates that he arrived at home on the 19th.

the few old men not reenlisted leave for home to be mustered out—

The rest of the Reg^t continues as a battalion of 6 or 7 Co^s and I of course shall not go in for 3 yrs more as Capt. of Inft^y having given up promotion for the sake of leaving the line—I might, to be sure, stay longer if I were one of the 3 aides allowed the Gen^{ls} by law but as I'm not and am liable to go back to the Regt if any change sh^d take place, I leave—If it should be necessary to go into the service again I should try for a commission from the Presd^t but I shan't bother myself ab^t that for the pres^t

Do you think I could get a place for my nagur boy if I brought him with me? Answer this last by the next mail after getting this—

Yr loving O W H, Jr

INDEX

Abbott, Henry L., 40, 41, 56, 60, 69, 70, 72, 74n., 76, 90-91, 94n., 105
Agassiz, Ida, 47
Allen's Farm, 58, 60-61
Alley, Leander F., 76
Amory, Charles, 94
Andrew Sharpshooters, 7, 39
Andrew, John A., 135, 143
Andrews, George L., 31
Antietam, Battle of, 62-66
Appleton, Nathan, 129
Aquia Creek, 72
Army and Navy Journal, 107, 128
Atlantic Monthly, The, 55
Averell, William A., 119
Ayres, Romeyn B., (C. G., 1st Brigade, 1st Division, Sixth Corps), 117, 118, 120

Babnew, ——, 137
Babo, Alvis, 18
Ball's Bluff, 13-33, 53, 127
Baltimore, Maryland, 4
Banks, Nathaniel P., 31
Barlow, Francis C., 114
Barnard, George M., Jr., 129
Bartlett, William Francis, 7, 8, 12nn., 38n., 41, 46-47, 104, 106
Bartlett, Mrs. W. F., *see* Pomeroy, Agnes
Baxter's Fire Zouaves, 26, 29
Beauregard, P. G. T., 138
Berdan, Hiram, 7
Bigelow, John, 129

Birney, David B., 115, 127
Boscovich, R. J., 95
Boston, Massachusetts, 71
Boston Daily Advertiser, 79
Brandy Station, 103
Brooke, John R., 90
Brown, Henry W., 102n., 104
Bull Run, First Battle of, 149
Burnside, Ambrose B., 69n., 85n., 108, 115, 116, 119, 126, 127, 128, 129, 130, 132, 141. *See also* Ninth Corps
Butler, Benjamin F., 119, 146

Cabot, Charles F., 41, 74-75
Cadwalader, Charles E., 126
Cairnes, J. E., *The Slave Power*, 81
Casey, Silas, 48
Casualties, 53, 56-57, 116-117
Catlett's Station, 69, 70, 71
Censorship, 12
Chancellorsville, Virginia, 103, 108
Chancellorsville campaign, 32, 92-93
Chickahominy River, 145
Civil War, progress of, 73, 79-80
Cold Harbor, 138-139
Comstock, C. B., 39, 41
Corcoran's Legion, 127
Correspondents, War, 149
Couch, Darius N., 85n.
Cowan, Andrew, 111, 112
Crowninshield, Caspar, 11
Curtis, Arthur R., 126

Dalton, Edward B., 108, 114
Dalton, Henry R., 105
Dana, Napoleon J. T., 32n., 37, 59
Death, contemplation of, 27, 32
Death, indifference to, 78
Dehon, Caroline Inches, 133, 144
Dixwell, Fanny Bowditch, 47, 101, 126, 128
Dreher, Ferdinand, 18, 29-30, 72
Drewry's Bluff, 119n.
Duffy, James N., 105, 134

Edwards Ferry, 9, 11, 29
Ely's Ford, 108
Everett, William, 143
Evil, nature of, 28
Ewell, R. S., 127, 130
Ewing, Charles, 101

Fair Oaks, Battle of, 47-52, 53, 62-63, 86, 89
Falmouth, Virginia, guard duty in, 79-91
Farrar, Henry W., 107, 128
Fifteenth Regiment, Mass. Volunteers, 53, 66
Fifth Corps, 103, 115, 117, 120. See also Warren, G. K.
Fifth Regiment, N. H. Volunteers, 58
Fifty-third Regiment, Pa. Volunteers, 90
Findlay, Anna Howell Kennedy, 67n.
First Division (Sixth Corps), 94n., 101-102, 109, 139, 145, 146. See also Russell, David A.
Folsom, Charles W., 94n.
Fort Darling, see Drewry's Bluff
Fort Independence, 3
Fort Pickens, 54

Forty-second Regiment, N. Y. Volunteers, 52, 53
Fourth Battalion (New England Guards), 3
Fourth Regiment, N. J. Volunteers, 101
Franklin, W. B., 77
Franklin, W. S., 138
Fraternization, Union and Confederate, 12, 44
Fredericksburg, Virginia, 69, 71, 72
Fredericksburg, Battle of, 40-41n., 74-79, 86-88, 90-91
Fredericksburg, Second Battle of, see Chancellorsville campaign
Fuller, Arthur B., 71, 76
Fuller, Margaret, 71, 76

Germana Ford, 103
Getty, George Washington (C. G., 2nd Division, Sixth Corps), 107n., 127n., 151. See also Second Division (Sixth Corps)
Gibbon, John (C. G., 2nd Division, Second Corps), 139, 146n. See also Second Division (Second Corps)
Glendale, Battle of, 58-60
Gordon, George H., 31
Gordon, John B., 107, 113n.
Grant, Lewis A. (C. O., 2nd Brigade, 2nd Division, Sixth Corps), 112n., 133
Grant, Ulysses S., 45n., 109n., 111, 131, 139
Griffin, Charles, 117, 131
Grosvenor, Ira R., 59
Gurney, Mrs. E. W., see Hooper, Ellen

Hagerstown, Maryland, 67-68
Hall, Norman J., 86, 90

Halleck, Henry W., 79
Hallowell, Anna, 126, 135, 137
Hallowell, Edward N., 41, 44
Hallowell, Emily, 70
Hallowell, Morris L., 5
Hallowell, Norwood Penrose, 5nn.,
18, 27, 29, 42, 43, 44, 45, 49, 51,
60, 65-66, 76
Hallowell, William Penrose, 31,
32
Hallowell family, 71
Hancock, W. S. (C. G., Second
Corps), 103, 105, 112, 113, 115,
116, 118, 125, 127, 130, 131, 132,
138, 139. *See also* Second Corps
Harper's Ferry, 63
Harper's Weekly, 149
Harris and Chapman, apothecaries,
63
Harrison's Landing, 56, 58, 108
Haven, S. Foster, Jr., 66
Haydn, T. L., 101, 113, 128
Hayward, Nathan, 25, 26, 30, 31,
76, 93, 133, 135, 141n.
Hibbard, Lansing E., 30
Higginson, Mrs. H. L., *see* Agas-
siz, Ida
Hill, Mrs. Adams Sherman, *see*
Dehon, Caroline Inches
Holmes, Amelia Jackson, 5, 44, 54,
70, 102, 144
Holmes, Edward Jackson, 5, 64,
103, 144
Holmes, Dr. Oliver Wendell, 3n.,
28, 64, 67, 79-80, 86, 95-97, 127,
135, 148
Holmes, Oliver Wendell, Jr., en-
listment and training, 3; commissioned 1st Lt., 20th Regiment,
4n.; first field experiences, 4-12;
poem by, 6, 12; Ball's Bluff, 13-
33, 127; religious scepticism, 27-
38; convalescence, 1861, 37n.;

Peninsula campaign, 38-61; attitude to war, 42, 64; health, 8,
11, 42, 44, 53, 54, 55, 61-62, 62-
63, 74, 141n.; promotion, 45-46,
135, 143, 152; relations with his
men, 53; morale, 8, 54, 60, 64,
79-80, 91, 122-123, 135, 143; Antietam, 62-68; convalescence,
1862, 67-68, 69n.; return to front,
Nov. '62, 69-73; attitude in so-
cial matters, 71; Fredericksburg,
74-79; drawing, 75; stationed at
Falmouth, Va., 79-91; photo-
graphs of, 12, 80; leave in Philadelphia, 85n.; possible staff ap-
pointments, 85-86; reading, 91;
wound in Chancellorsville campaign, 92-93; assignment to First
Division, Sixth Corps, 94n.; diaries, 101, 103; Wilderness campaign, 102-107; intention to resign, 122, 135, 142-143; exploit
with message, 133-134, 136-137,
142; Spottsylvania campaign, 108-
127; Rapidan to James, 128-146;
staff and line duty compared,
142; discharge, 151-152
Hooker, Joseph, 63, 85n.
Hooper, Ellen, 61
Hovey, ——, 31
Humphreys, A. A., 111, 126, 129

Immortality, 27-28

Jackson, Elizabeth Cabot, 141
James River, 60, 145-146
Johnson, Edward, 116n.
Johnson, William A., 60
Jones, Ellen, 67n.

Kelliher, John, 126
Kent, J. Ford, 117

Kershaw, Joseph B., 58
Kirby, Edmund, 48n.

Lander, Frederick W., 7, 8
LeDuc, W. G., 65-66n., 77
Lee, Robert E., 103, 108, 113
Lee, William Raymond, 7, 13, 18, 32n., 37n., 59, 72-73n., 85n.
Leech, ——, 77
Letters, eagerness for, 12, 42, 44-45, 52, 54, 60, 64, 123
Lincoln, Abraham, 54
Longstreet, James, 109, 130, 138
Lowell, James Jackson, 18, 51, 56, 60
Lyman, Theodore, 114, 126

Mackenzie, Ranald S., 117
McCartney, William H., 107, 109, 111, 112
McClellan, Arthur, 133
McClellan, George B., 38, 44, 63n., 80, 150
McGregor, Fanny, 47, 74, 144
McKay, Thomas M., 33n., 75
McLaws, Lafayette, 138
McMahon, Martin T., 110, 133
Macy, George N., 74n., 76, 85n., 90, 105
Mallon, James E., 85
Malvern Hill, 60, 61
Marryat, Frederick, Children of the New Forest, 24
Mason, Herbert C., 72, 76
Mathematical problem, 95-97
Meade, George G., 109, 110, 111, 112, 116, 118, 128, 131, 133, 139, 150
Merchant, John, 18, 24, 25
Metropolitan Hotel, 33
Milton, William F., 77
Morale, Union, 39, 43, 51, 52, 53, 64, 73, 79-80, 149-150

Morris, W. H., Field Tactics, 101
Morse, John T., Jr., 55
Motley, John Lothrop, 79
Mott, Gersham (C. G., 4th Division, Second Corps), 111, 113, 115, 116, 118
Müller, August, 57, 60
Murphy, James, 53-54, 76, 93

National Hotel, 33, 37, 61
Negro troops, 148-149
Neill, Thomas H. (C. G., 3rd Brigade, 2nd Division, Sixth Corps), 107, 112, 124, 127, 128, 131-132, 139
Nelson's Farm, battle at, 58-59, 61
New England Guards, see Fourth Battalion (New England Guards)
New York City, 4, 127
New York Herald, 63
New York Tribune, 106, 107, 149
Niles, ——, 3
Nineteenth Regiment, Mass. Volunteers, 7, 52
Ninth Corps, 145. See also Burnside, Ambrose B.
Noonan, John, 59
Norton, Charles Eliot, 122n.

Oehlenschlager, Dr., 128
One Hundred and Twenty-first Regiment, N. Y. Volunteers, 102
O'Sullivan, John, 26, 29, 33

Page, Charles A., 105n., 149
Paine, Sumner, 92
Palfrey, Francis W., 37, 41, 45-46, 59, 60, 72-73n., 77, 85n.
Patten, Henry L., 56, 60, 76, 80
Peirson, Charles L., 32
Peninsula campaign, 38-61, 64, 108
Penrose, William H., 117

Perkins, William F., 76
Perry, George B., 3
Perry, John G., 133
Petersburg campaign, 146-151
Pettigrew, James J., 50
Philadelphia, Pa., 4, 31, 37, 46, 71, 93
Piney Branch Church, 108
Pittsburgh Landing, see Shiloh, Battle of
Pomeroy, Agnes, 12, 143n.
Pomeroy, Maria Center, 12
Pomeroy, Robert, 5, 12
Potter, Alonzo, 86
Potter, James Nelson, 86
Profanity, 28-29
Putnam, John C., 18, 25, 31, 38
Putnam, William Lowell, 18, 26, 31, 60

Rappahanock Station, 108
Religion, 27-28
Revere, Paul Joseph, 58, 66, 85n.
Rhodes, William B., 112
Rice, ——, 103
Rice, James C., 107
Ricketts' Battery, 48-49
Ricketts, James B. (C. G., 3rd Division, Sixth Corps), 110, 124, 125, 127, 128, 131, 139, 149. See also Third Division (Sixth Corps)
Robie, Frederick, 94
Ropes, Henry, 76, 85
Russell, David A. (C. G., 1st Division, Sixth Corps), 101n., 104, 107, 111, 112, 116, 123, 127, 128, 131, 132, 133, 134, 144, 145. See also First Division (Sixth Corps)

Salient, The, 115-117, 125
Saunders, John, 7n., 39
Savage's Station, 58, 60-61

Schmitt, George A., 18
Seaver, Thomas O., 124
Secession, 73, 79-80
Second Corps, 139, 148. See also Hancock, W. S.
Second Division (Second Corps), 148. See also Gibbon, John
Second Division (Sixth Corps), 145-146. See also Getty, George Washington
Second Regiment, Mass. Volunteers, 31
Sedgwick, John, 9n., 32n., 37, 85-86, 104, 106, 107, 108, 109-110
Seven Days Battle, 56-61
Seventh Regiment, Mich. Volunteers, 59
Seventy-second Regiment, Pa. Volunteers, 26, 29
Seward, William H., 79
Seymour, Truman, 106, 113
Shaler, Alexander, 102, 104, 106
Shenandoah Valley, 119n.
Shepard, Allen, 72-73
Sheridan, Philip, 113, 120, 132
Shields, James, 25
Shiloh, Battle of, 45
Sixteenth Regiment, Mass. Volunteers, 71
Sixth Corps, 94n., 110, 115. See also Sedgwick, John; Wright, Horatio G.
Sixth Regiment, Maine Volunteers, 101
Sixty-fifth Regiment, N. Y. Volunteers, 102
Slavery, 80
Slemmer, Adam J., 54
Smith, Henry J., 13, 23
Smith, William F., 138, 139, 148-149
South Mountain, Battle of, 63
Southerners, attitude of, 72, 80

Spottsylvania, Campaign at, 108-127
Spottsylvania Court House, 108
Steuart, George H., 116n.
Stevensburg, 103
Stevenson, T. G., 3
Stragglers, 72, 103, 130
Stuart, J. E. B., 120
Sturgis, Henry H., 27, 28-29, 30
Sumner, Edwin V., 37, 63n., 73, 74, 85n., 138
Sydney, Sir Philip, 24

Tactics, 101
Tammany Regiment, see Forty-second Regiment, N. Y. Volunteers
Tennallytown, Maryland, 62
Tenth Regiment, Mass. Volunteers, 53, 124
Tenth Regiment, N. J. Volunteers, 116
Third Division (Sixth Corps), 139, 140, 145-146. See also Ricketts, James B.
Third Regiment, Vermont Volunteers, 124
Thirty-fourth Regiment, N. Y. Volunteers, 49
Tompkins, Charles H., 133
Torbert, A. T. A., 100, 132
Tremlett, Henry M., 8, 11, 23, 31, 37, 60
Twentieth Regiment, Mass. Volunteers, 4n., 52-53, 59, 61n., 72-73, 85n., 86, 90-91, 105-106, 122, 126, 135, 148, 151-152
Tyler, Mason W., 112
Tyler, R. O., 127

Upton, Emory (C. O., 2nd Brigade, 1st Division, Sixth Corps), 102, 104, 109, 112-113, 118, 121, 134, 146

Walleston, Edmund A., 11, 31
Walton, Charles Morris, 5, 12
Warren, G. K. (C. G., Fifth Corps), 103, 109, 112, 116, 117, 127, 128, 129, 130, 131, 132, 138. See also Fifth Corps
Warrenton, Virginia, 69, 70, 71
Washington, D. C., 4, 7, 33, 37, 61-62, 63, 70, 151n.
Waud, Alfred R., 149
Wesselhoeft, Reinhold, 18
Wheaton, Frank, 127, 128
White House, The, 33
Whittier, Charles A., 9, 19, 25, 26, 27, 29, 85, 105, 109-110, 137n., 139-140n.
Wiebecke, Charles, 118
Wilderness campaign, 40n., 102-107
Wilkins, Henry E., 30-31
Willard, Samuel, 76
Willard's Hotel, 33
Winsor, Henry, 132
Winsor, Mrs. Henry, see Jackson, Elizabeth Cabot
Wright, Chauncey, 5
Wright, Horatio, G., 9n., 94, 104, 105, 106, 107, 108, 109, 110, 112, 115, 116, 118, 119, 126, 127, 128, 129, 132, 133, 139, 142, 148
Wright, James Edward, 5

Young, ——, 129